Word Processing

Other titles in this series

Word Processing

Barbara Shaw, BA, DipInstM, is a Senior Lecturer in the Business
and Management Department, Oldham College of Technology. She
teaches word processing and Business Studies on a variety of
courses and has a particular interest in integrating word processing
and information technology into the teaching of business and
management studies.

Word Processing

Barbara Shaw

Consultant Editor: Joyce Stananought

Chambers *Commerce Series*

© Barbara Shaw 1987

Published by W & R Chambers Ltd Edinburgh, 1987

British Library Cataloguing in Publication Data

Shaw, Barbara
   Word processing.—(Chambers commerce
series).
   1. Word processing—Problems, exercises, etc.
   I.Title
   652'.5'076   HF5548.115

ISBN 0-550-20707-4

Typeset by Waddie & Co. Ltd Edinburgh

Printed in Great Britain by
Richard Clay Ltd, Bungay, Suffolk

Contents

PART VI   ADDITIONAL WORD PROCESSING FUNCTIONS

Chapter 7   Listing and Merging, Search and Replace, Pagination

PART VII   APPLICATIONS OF WORD PROCESSING

Chapter 8   The Applications of Word Processing in Various Organisations

Acknowledgements

It is not possible to write a book without a great deal of help from other people. I should like therefore to record a sincere thank you to all my students, both past and present, from whom I have accumulated a great many ideas and much useful information — particularly those students who use a word processor and also manage word processing centres in their daily jobs. I should also like to thank my colleagues at Oldham College of Technology and particularly Derek McKeown, the Head of Department of Business and Management, for his managerial support and encouragement when word processing was first introduced into the College. Thanks are also due to colleagues on the word processing moderating panel at the North Western Regional Advisory Council; also to NWRAC for allowing me to reproduce some of the examination papers; and finally to my husband for his continued support and help whilst I was writing this book.

Preface

This book is a guide to word processing. Having taught the subject for some years to a variety of age ranges I would like to think that it is a guide that can be used as a self-teaching text. It has been written strictly in the sequence in which I would teach.

Whilst a book will never replace a teacher, in all practical subjects it is the learner who does most of the teaching through their own practical application. Because of the large number of word processing systems on the market I have attempted to explain and demonstrate general concepts, which are broken down into individual sections each containing practical assignments.

The book therefore aims to familiarise the complete beginner to word processing with the key concepts and practices, and to provide assignments which can be used either by the complete beginner or by the word processing operator who, having learnt one system, has to transfer that knowledge to another. In this instance this book should be used in conjunction with the operator's manual and all the practical assignments should be attempted on the new machine.

B. S.

AN INTRODUCTION
TO WORD PROCESSING

When people see a word processor for the first time, they are often amazed and delighted by the ease of operation, which is made to look that much easier by the skill of the demonstrator. The student therefore assumes that it is easy to learn, but like most skills, and the typist knows all about skills, the learning comes with practice.

The typist will be familiar with the keyboard, which is usually the same as that on a typewriter, but most typists will be unfamiliar with the disk drives and the use of floppy disks.

The appearance of the word processor therefore is somewhat alien even to typists, and the biggest barrier to using it is switching it on and actually loading the program; this is known as 'booting up' the system.

Try using the following sequence as a guide, but take care to follow the specific manufacturer's instructions as well.

1   Check that the disk drive and the printer are connected to the *main unit*. The main unit consists of the *screen (visual display unit or VDU)* and the *keyboard*.

2   Switch on the main unit.

3   Insert the manufacturer's program or operating disk into the disk drive and either close the door or press the button.

4   The machine should now 'read' the program disk, a red light often indicates that this is taking place. It is important that the disk drive door is not opened nor the disk removed whilst the red indicator light is glowing. It is also important that the machine or the electricity supplying it is not switched off at this point, because if this should happen the program disk could be damaged.

5   On some machines the program disk can be removed once it has been read into the memory and the warning light is no longer displayed. The program should now be in the memory of the machine and will stay there until the power is switched off at the mains, or the machine is switched off.

6   Depending upon the particular machine and program, the screen will now show either a blank page with the left and right margins at the extreme edges of the screen; alternatively the screen will show a *menu*.

7   A menu is another name for help instructions and as in any menu, choices have to be made; but instead of a choice of dishes, this menu gives a choice of operations which the operator may want to perform, e.g. 'create a document', or 'edit a file'. In the case of more recent word processors, the menu offers a choice of document layouts, known as templates. These include such preset layouts as memos, letters or reports.

   The most that is required of the operator at this point is to press a single key which is usually indicated on the menu, e.g. C for create a document or D to open a file. However, if the program does not separate these two, it sometimes merely asks, 'name of file to edit'? This is the next barrier to overcome, because the operator feels that they do not know the name of this mystery file.

8   The mystery arises because the machine assumes that a file already exists and wants to know the name. The new operator also assumes that they should know the name of this file.

9   The operator should type in a name. The number of letters or figures allowed in the name will vary from machine to machine; for instance, some machines limit the name to eight to eleven characters. Some machines will not accept a full stop in the middle of the name, whereas others demand a name followed by a number. The operator's manual should indicate this, but a suggestion is made that perhaps the first document typed could be called 'first' and 001 if a number is required. At the time of creating a document a coded or shortened name may be meaningful to the operator and indicate clearly the contents of the document, but several weeks later when the operator returns to edit this document it may be difficult to remember the significance that was apparent at the time of creating it.

10 After keying in most commands, the operator is required to execute these, by pressing either the carriage return or the enter or execute key. Such a key will need to be pressed after typing in the name of a document. Most machines respond by

acknowledging the command and showing 'new file'. This is often the first communication between the machine and the operator.

On most machines preset margins will be all that are needed for the first exercise. The operator should not try to change these at present because the objective of this initial lesson is:

(i) to become familiar with the cursor movements;

(ii) to practise typing on the screen instead of on paper;

(iii) to practise typing without using the carriage return at the ends of lines.

PART I
THE MACHINE AND ITS OPERATION

Chapter 1

Word Processing Introduced

1.1 Cursor and Function Keys

The cursor on a word processor denotes the typing point, and it is indicated by a highlighted block, the same size as any one of the characters appearing on the screen. This block may flash or remain static but it is usually repeated directly above its position on the format line (the line which shows the margin settings and tabulator settings), sometimes referred to as the ruler line.

Cursor

The cursor, just like the typing point on a typewriter, can be moved from left to right, and right to left. This is achieved on a typewriter by using the back-space key to go from right to left and the space bar to move from left to right. On a typewriter it is necessary to use the roller or platen to move up and the line spacer or carriage return to move down the page. The cursor on a word processor can be moved in all four directions, usually by pressing keys marked with arrows to denote the direction.

These arrow keys are usually found on the keypad at the right-hand side of the letter keyboard. It is necessary to press each arrow key once in order to move one space in each direction. However, it is possible to keep the key depressed and the cursor will continue to move in the direction of its arrow until it is released. This is known as 'scrolling'.

On some machines there is an extra cursor key, known as the quick cursor key which works in conjunction with the other cursor keys. Instead of keeping the left arrow key pressed down when it is required to return to the left margin, the operator presses the cursor key marked ↖ (the quick cursor key), then the left arrow key. This makes the cursor jump back to the left margin. Alternatively, the diagonal arrow key can be pressed twice and the typing point (cursor) will return to the first letter on the document, usually this is positioned on the top line and starts at the left hand margin.

It should be mentioned here that some operators who are using a word processing program on a computer, otherwise known as a 'word processing package', may find it necessary to press a control key and one of the letter keys at the same time in order to move the typing point in either direction. Four different letter keys will be used in conjunction with the control key, in order to move in each of the four directions, up, down, left and right.

Before beginning to type, the operator should practise moving the cursor keys in all four directions.

The next step is merely to type upon the screen and resist the temptation to press the carriage return at the end of each line, allowing the machine to wrap around the words automatically.

The carriage return is pressed twice when a new paragraph is required and a symbol on the screen will appear to show the operator where new paragraphs have been started. This symbol may appear on the screen as ◁ or ↵. The new operator will undoubtedly find a few other barriers to learning in the initial stages, but it may help to note that these areas are the ones known to cause difficulty at first simply because of the variety of systems and machines on the market and small differences in operation in each of them. Some of these areas include:

(i) switching on and booting up the system (see Introduction);

(ii) printing out the documents (see Section 2.3);

(iii) erasing the screen and exiting from a document (see Section 1.5).

All these functions will of course be explained in the operator's manual but they may not be given in the sequence expected or under the most obvious headings and titles.

Function keys

Most word processors and computers have an extra keypad which is positioned to the right or the left of the qwerty keyboard. On some machines the keys are marked with the function they perform, e.g. 'char del' or 'relay', 'execute' 'insert'. However, some keys are merely marked F1, F2, F3, F4, F5 etc. and one key may incorporate two functions, e.g. F1 and F2. F1 is engaged when the machine is in lower case and the same key pressed in upper case gives F2.

In the early stages of learning to use the machine the operator may find it difficult to remember what function F1 performs. Therefore some word processing programs include an explanation of these which appears on the top of the screen as part of the menu. This may read:

F1–lines, F2–services, F3–layout, F4–quit

Another way to assist the operator to remember is to use an 'overlay'. This is simply a piece of plastic with cut-outs which fits over the keys but in effect labels the key at the side with the same information that would be presented on a screen menu. Whichever method is used the operator still has to remember what function key F2–services will perform.

The number and operation of each function key will vary with each machine and even though operators may find they are using the same word processing program on two similar machines, that is the same hardware and software, the function keys can still vary–because some word processing programs allow the operator to program the function keys. By this we mean, if the hardware has a set of function keys which are not in use then instead of the control key and the letters OC being pressed to centre a line of text, a function key can be set up and programmed to do just this. This may be function key F7.

If the function keys are programmed by the operators then it is important that everyone using the machines knows which function keys are programmed to perform which task. Therefore from a supervisory angle it is advisable for all the machines to be set up in the same way and a 'key' to the functions made available to each operator; alternatively a home-made template may be prepared and placed on each machine.

1.2 Operator Manuals

No doubt all manufacturers feel they provide in their manuals an adequate and explicit guide to the use of their product, and no doubt many operators feel they could do better, after having to spend several hours or even weeks working painstakingly through it.

The manual could be the pride and joy of the marketing department. If it is, then the chances are that the instructions will be relatively easy to follow. However, if the systems analyst or computer software writer has been given the task of compiling it then this could be a different matter. The major reasons for this are as follows:

1   Those in the marketing department through their training should write with the customer in mind. They will have practical experience of explaining and demonstrating the machine to their potential customers. Possibly they will have learnt from the many questions asked of them just what the customer/user is looking for in the operation of the machine. Also it is the marketing department's sole objective to sell the machine.

   The program writer's job is to write the program and at the end of the task they will be so familiar with it that they may overlook points which the customer may find difficult to grasp.

2   The marketing personnel should be skilled in written communication.

The buyer is not going to know for certain who wrote the manual—but nevertheless will come to love or loathe the great 'tome' which will become his or her daily companion for some time to come.

1.3 Compile Your Own Manual

In order to speed up the learning process and remove the necessity to refer continually to the 'great tome', learners and new operators should compile their own manual.

This can take the form of a small notebook which is indexed into pages in alphabetical order. Every time a new instruction or command is learnt the new operator should enter the instructions for this command under the appropriate letter page. For instance the command for deleting a word could be listed under 'D' for delete together with all the other commands which refer to deleting. The command for moving text could be listed under 'M' and so on.

This notebook will serve not only as a very useful and personalised guide, it will also help to reinforce the instructions in the operator's own memory. It will provide that 'back-up copy' in case the operator's permanent 'store' is switched off, as it is with many of us, during relaxation at weekends or when on holiday. Human beings, like computers, sometimes need to be reprogrammed upon their return to work and this notebook should serve that purpose.

Another problem which word processing operators often come across, is that of the operating manual referring to different operations by different titles, so what one operator may mean by 'search and replace' could be shown in the manual as 'find and exchange'. Although this would be a fairly obvious instruction to decipher, such topics as 'reformat' on one machine may be listed as 'tab indent' on another. The notebook can be used here to cross-reference such instructions.

1.4 Status and Format Lines

Upon beginning to use a word processor for the first time, new operators are often frustrated by the fact that the screen is not entirely blank—indeed on some systems nearly 50% of the screen is covered with instructions in the form of a menu. Most screens will have at least two lines occupied at the top of the screen, these being the 'format line', sometimes referred to as the 'ruler line', and the 'status line'.

The format line shows the margin settings and any tabular settings or indentations. The margins are often denoted by L for left and R for right with T for tabulator settings and I for indents.

The status line is the information line and it is this line which indicates to the operator which commands have been enacted and the stage and sequence in the setting of them. That is, if the print command has been given this will be shown as 'Print' followed by a - - - - - or a ? to indicate that only half of the command has been received and the machine is awaiting a further instruction, e.g. does the operator want to print from screen or from disk? This part of the status line is known as the message section and it is this which is of most help to the operator and the part which the operator must learn to read and check and use in their interaction with the machine. Another section of the status line shows the mode of operation being used: e.g. 'I' may indicate that the machine is in 'insert mode', 'J' may indicate that the justification is switched on and a small line _ may show that the machine is in automatic underlining mode.

A further section of the status line may refer to the state of the peripherals, i.e. the disk drives and printers and whether or not these are engaged.

The status line also indicates the width of the video screen and the pre-page length set, i.e. the horizontal and vertical dimensions of the screen; it also shows the current line position, so if the cursor is taken down to line 10 on the screen, the status line may read V10.

Character setting, i.e. pitch, and line spacing are also shown on this line.

1.5 Video Screen Page

The size of the screen or VDU varies according to the system. Many screens display 80 characters or columns across and approximately 25 lines down. It is possible to buy a screen which will display a full A4-size sheet of paper. These machines are, however, used mostly for work of an intricate nature such as the typing of theses that may include large numbers of formulae with subscripts and superscripts, or for the preparation of elaborate displays. Nevertheless it should be remembered that even with a screen which displays only 80 characters across and 25 lines down, it is possible for the operator to see more than would be seen on a conventional typewriter, when the paper does not stand up at right angles and much of it disappears around the platen.

On a word processor, although the video screen shows 80 characters across it does not mean that a wider typing line cannot be used. As mentioned in the section on tabulation it is possible to extend the amount of text on one line to 200 or more characters, simply by increasing the horizontal setting, and as the eightieth character is approached, the text to the left of the screen 'falls off' making space for the next 80 characters. This can be retrieved at any time by the operator scrolling, i.e. moving the cursor back to the left so that the text returns to the screen and the text on the right-hand side disappears. So although it is not possible to see all 200 characters at a glance, by simply scrolling across line by line all 200 characters can be typed and read.

Once the operator has actually started to type on the screen and has mastered the cursor movements, using a word processor is little different from typing on a piece of paper. However, one cannot continue typing for long before either the end of the screen page length is reached (if the system is so configured) or alternatively the system automatically shows the end of one page by displaying a broken line - - - - - - - across the screen indicating to the operator that one page has been completed and it is beginning another one. When the operator wants to exit the document, some systems allow the operator to save the document automatically on disk or give the choice of 'Save and Print', 'Abandon Document', or 'Save and Continue'.

It is suggested that at this stage of training you should learn only how to erase the screen and abandon the document. If the system is menu-driven—that is, the instructions appear on the screen—it will be a simple matter to press the keys shown and abandon the document.

However, there is always a grave temptation at this point to ignore the instructions and merely switch off the machine and start again. Although this achieves the objective of clearing the screen you must remember that if you do this then you have to reprogram the system and go through all the procedure of booting it up again.

Exercise 1 Keying in

Without attempting to change the preset margins, simply type the following passage. Remember, do not press the carriage return at the end of each line; press this only when a new paragraph is needed.

Do not press the space bar to move across the screen; use the cursor instead. Press the space bar only to indicate a space between words. Ignore any errors you may make.

Many people assume that word processing is of use only to a typist. This is not true. Word processors have enabled non-typists to produce typewritten material without the help of a typist. Word processors have become invaluable to the small businessman who wants to type the odd letter or the student who wishes to produce a typewritten assignment. However, until the machine is programmed to accept verbal commands, the operator will have to press keys and because the typist usually uses eight fingers and a non-typist uses just the two index fingers, it means that the typist has the advantage of speed in addition to the flexibility of word processing.

The professional word processing operator is also trained in the layout of the printed word and therefore a document which is produced by a trained operator is of a much higher standard.

1.6 Margins

It is now necessary to learn how to change the preset margins to the margins of your choice. These will need to be set to suit the type and size of stationery to be used. However, it is generally accepted practice to leave at least 1″ or 25 mm margins on A4 paper and not less than ½″ or 12 mm on A5 paper.

Many organisations may want to line up the margin settings with their printed letter headings.

It is suggested that after the explanation on margin settings has been read, the operator's manual should be consulted and different margin settings used.

Although the actual keys pressed to set the left- and right-hand margins will vary from system to system, the principles on most machines follow closely those of setting the margins on a typewriter, whereby the typing point (this being the cursor on the word processor, remember), is positioned at the appropriate number on the scale or the format line and then a command is pressed, to set the margin. These commands will vary from pressing OL for the left margin and OR for the right margin to pressing a special format key followed by L for left and then R for right; or on some systems, a special function key is given this job.

At the acceptance of the command, the format line will show a permanent letter L and letter R at the positions of the margin settings, until these are changed. The selection of the appropriate number for the setting will depend upon the 'pitch' (pitch is another word meaning size of type), to which the machine is set. The pitch can be 15 characters to the inch (microtype) or 12 characters to the inch (elite type) or 10 characters to the inch (pica type).

Once the margins are set, all typescript should appear within this framework. Although it is possible on many systems to type outside the left and right hand margins, it is not possible to insert or delete whilst in the margins. The letters typed in the margins, will, however, be printed.

In considering margin settings, therefore, we can see that:

(i)   on most systems it is merely a matter of positioning the cursor at the left margin setting and pressing a key and then positioning the cursor at the right margin setting and pressing a key;

(ii) to change margin settings in the middle of a piece of work it is sometimes necessary to do this before the text is typed by bringing down the ruler line and resetting the margins;

(iii) alternatively some systems allow the operator to change the margin setting after the text has been typed and this is known as reformatting.

1.7 Pitch

From the previous pages, you should remember that pitch means the size of type.

The change in character size is not shown on the screen of a word processor, i.e. the letters all appear to be the same size no matter what pitch is used so that the effect can be seen only when the document is printed out. However, if the operator uses a 10 pitch, the letters typed will be bigger and if the margins have not been set correctly, the printing may run off the edge of the paper. Therefore it is necessary to set or select the pitch before setting the margins and before beginning to type.

Some systems actually have a menu to help the operator. This gives a list of the pitch sizes i.e. 10 pitch, 12 pitch, 15 pitch, and the cursor is placed over the selected pitch followed by the execute key and the pitch is set. Other systems require the operator to press the format key followed by a number, corresponding to the size of pitch. Or a special function key may be programmed to change the pitch. The operator's manual will need to be consulted for each machine.

The choice of pitch will depend upon the document being typed. If it is necessary to fit a large amount of typing on to one page, e.g. when typing out instructions for the use of a machine and you want to use one page instead of two, then a pitch of 15 characters to the inch, i.e. micro-type, may be chosen. A thin booklet as compared to a larger manual may convince the buyer of the machine that it is less complicated to operate than it is. Some word processing manuals are an example of this use of small type; they often look like small innocent volumes which can be read and understood in a matter of hours. Do not be deceived.

However, if it is important that your document is easy to read then a larger pitch of 10 characters to the inch would be more appropriate.

Size of type

If using a daisy wheel printer a different pitch can be achieved by changing the printer code and the daisy wheel. The standard size is 12 characters to the inch (elite type). Ten characters to the inch is pica type and 15 characters to the inch is micro type. However, on some machines it is possible to achieve character sizes between and below these standard variations e.g. 11 character spaces to the inch. The size of type is often changed for display purposes. For example lecture notes may contain quotations and in order to show that these quotations are not the lecturer's own notes, a different style or character size may be used for the quotation to distinguish it from the lecturer's own notes.

Typefaces

On a daisy wheel printer, different typefaces can be achieved by simply changing the daisy wheel. However, if a dot matrix printer is used, the situation becomes more complicated. In some systems commands can be sent to the printer which will alter the typeface, the commands having to be embedded with the text, i.e. by using a printer code, or by typing in a set of instructions before word processing begins.

It is difficult to generalise with dot matrix printers, since the facility to use different typefaces is not only dependent upon the complexity of the printer itself but also upon the ability of the word processing program to pass any command which may be needed to the printer.

Proportional spacing

In order to give the appearance of a professionally printed document, many word processors can perform proportional spacing. This means that the space allowed between each letter is made equal. In non-proportional spacing the space after a letter 'i' would be greater than the space left after the letter 'm' simply because 'm' takes up more space than 'i'. However, to do proportional spacing a word processor often requires that a special proportional spaced daisy wheel is inserted into the printer. After this has been done, all the operator has to do is to insert the appropriate codes wherever the proportional spacing should start and end.

Proportional spacing would give a professional appearance to the Chairman's Report that is circulated to all shareholders at the Annual General Meeting.

1.8 Printers

The following types of printers are the most commonly used for printing out the work produced on word processors: daisy wheel printers, dot matrix printers and laser printers. These vary in price, quality of print produced and the speed at which they operate.

Daisy wheel printers

This is possibly the most commonly used type of printer for word processing, because it gives a quality finish which is similar and in many cases superior to that finish which is produced on a typewriter. However, daisy wheel printers are more expensive than dot matrix printers and they also operate more slowly, even though many of them are capable of bi-directional printing, i.e. printing from left to right and then instead of the print head returning to the left and starting to print again, it prints on its return from right to left also.

The actual daisy wheel itself is made of plastic and as the name implies has petals, each one containing a character. These print wheels are subject to wear and tear and can be bought relatively cheaply, i.e. from £5 to £12 depending upon the type.used. The daisy wheel therefore is considered a consumable.

Laser printers

These printers give a very high quality finish and operate relatively quietly and at extremely high speeds. In appearance they look like a photocopying machine. Laser printers vary in price according to the speed of their operation. A laser printer which is capable of producing 250+ pages per minute may cost in the region of £25 000 whereas a much smaller desk-top laser printer which can produce 15-25 pages per minute may be purchased for as little as £2000. As sales of all laser printers increase so too will their costs reduce.

Dot matrix printers

A dot matrix printer is a printer which can be used to produce hard copies from a word processor instead of a daisy wheel printer or laser printer. An example of the print which is obtained when work is printed out on a dot matrix printer is shown below.

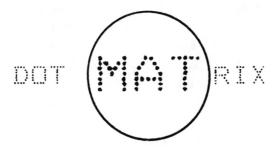

As is evident upon close examination, each character is made up of a series of dots, thereby giving a slightly mottled effect to the formation of the letters. This can be lessened by giving an instruction to the printer via the word processing program to overstrike the letters a second time, however, this slows down the printer considerably.

Some organisations consider that the print obtained from using a dot matrix printer is unacceptable for correspondence going outside the organisation. They may use a dot matrix printer for such items as drafts of minutes of meetings, or other internal correspondence.

Dot matrix printers are much cheaper than daisy wheel printers and can actually achieve a faster rate of print; they are also able to produce graphical displays. Because of the price they are very popular for use with home computers and word processors and also in training establishments and in schools.

1.9 Special Print Functions

Many word processing programs contain instructions for performing special print functions, and accept codes which activate the printer to produce bold type, or double underlining, or type which is not aligned with the rest of the text (above the normal typing line—superscripts, or below the line—subscripts), or characters which are overstruck and other variations of print. The operator is reminded, however, that even though the word processing program contains these functions the printer and also the print wheel must be capable of producing such effects.

In some instances, particularly where the word processing system is integrated into the total computerised system, either because of speed of operation or for economy reasons, the printer chosen does not always perform such tasks, therefore the word processing functions go to waste. The printer chosen often depends upon the primary use of the system. If word processing is central to this and the objective is to produce printed material of a high quality then the printer will be able to perform all the tasks which the word processing program can perform. Therefore, before using the special print functions, the operator should consult the systems manual as well as the printer manual and check:

(i) what functions the printer can produce and

(ii) if the print wheel needs to be changed prior to giving a special print command.

Although the codes and instructions used to obtain these special effects will vary with each system, the following are some of the types of print which can be achieved, together with some applications of them.

Bold type

This is sometimes called emboldening or emphasis type. The print head strikes the ribbon two or three times in order to print each character, and as a consequence a darker finish is produced. Bold type is used to make words or special headings stand out from the rest of the text in an attempt to focus the reader's attention on to certain aspects. Subscribers to business classified directories pay an extra fee in order to have their name and address emboldened because they feel that this will draw the buyer's attention to their name before the rest of the subscribers in the list who are offering a similar service.

Some job candidates use bold type in their curriculum vitae to emphasise their qualifications or certain aspects of their experience which they feel will be particularly relevant to the post in question.

Emboldening is often used as a display technique to emphasise items in leaflets or promotional material or in notices of meetings to emphasise the date of the meeting.

In reports certain words can be emphasised to stress their importance, e.g. 'this material is **confidential** and upon no account must it be circularised'.

The portion of text to be emboldened whether this is one word or one line or several lines needs to be indicated both at the beginning and at the end of it, and this is often done by placing a special printer code at the beginning and also one at the end to denote where the bold type is to start and finish.

Double underlining

The prime use of double underlining is in typing accounts where the final totals in invoices, trial balances, profit and loss accounts, income and expenditure accounts and balance sheets are doubly underlined in order to distinguish the final totals from the sub-totals. Again a code is placed at the beginning of the double underlining.

Subscripts and superscripts

Operators familiar with the periodic table used in chemistry will recognise the following symbols which require the use of the print functions which will make the characters appear above or below the line of type. On the screen the characters may appear on one line but when a code is placed before the character to be raised or lowered, the printed copy will show the superscripts above the line and the subscripts below the line. The use of superscripts and subscripts, therefore, is primarily in the typing of formulae. An example of both a subscript and superscript is given below:

$$CO_2 \qquad\qquad Ca^{2+}$$

1.10 Line Spacing

Most word processors offer a choice of line spacing which includes the conventional single, double and treble line spacing, with some offering 1½ or 2½ line spacing and other gradations.

Most machines default to single line spacing. Default means the return of the line and character settings to those which are part of the programmed instructions, i.e. most machines are automatically set to produce work both on the screen and on the hard copy in single line spacing unless otherwise instructed via a print command to change this.

Single line spacing is most commonly used for general correspondence, reports, minutes of meetings and memos. However double line spacing is used to produce drafts so that the author can write amendments between the lines.

The line spacing being used is indicated to the operator on the status line, which often shows a number to represent this. Single line spacing may be shown as S1, double line spacing as S2, and so on.

To change from single line spacing to double may mean that the operator has to select a particular style menu by pressing a function key, e.g. F5, when a menu will appear on the screen. The options offered for the style are presented, e.g.

underlined type   line spacing   bold type

The cursor is positioned over the line displaying 'line spacing' followed by a number. This may be 2 for double line spacing and 3 for treble, followed by the execute key. The acceptance of this command will be shown somewhere on the screen, either on the status line or at the top of the text. However, the actual text on the screen will remain in single line spacing but when printed out will be produced in the selected line spacing.

Even dedicated word processing systems, which allow the operator to change the line spacing prior to typing the task, may not display the text on the screen in double line spacing.

One point for the operator to remember about this of course is that whilst the machine is in single line spacing the vertical line count allows them to type up to 54 lines before paging the document or before the page divider is shown on the screen—when in double line spacing logically this paging should happen at approximately line 27, i.e. half of 54. However, this is not always so. Therefore if a document is typed in double line spacing and the operator types up to 54 lines of type on one page, this will not fit on to a sheet of A4 paper when printed in double line spacing.

On most word processing systems it is possible to have a document typed in double line spacing with just a section typed in single line spacing and vice versa.

This may be achieved by using a special printer code placed before and after the paragraph to be typed in a different spacing to the rest of the text. However, if the document is to be typed in single spacing and only two or three lines need to be typed in double line spacing then the easiest way to do this is to insert two carriage returns at the end of each line of type. The following examples serve to illustrate where it may be sensible to change the line spacing in the middle of a document.

1   In the preparation of a report in draft format the major part of this would initially be typed in double line spacing so that amendments can be made by each person who is a party to the report. However, if accounts form part of the report then these are more easily read if they are typed in single line spacing, whereas the rest of the report would be typed in double line spacing.

2   Another example is in the preparation of programmes or the Order of Service for a wedding. Whilst the programme may generally be typed in double line spacing a verse or a prayer would traditionally appear in single line spacing.

Test Yourself

1   Give another name for the term 'pitch'.
2   How many characters to the inch does elite type produce?
3   Give two examples when emboldening or bold type may be used.
4   What are subscripts?
5   What are superscripts?
6   What does the term default mean?
7   Where are the margin settings usually shown on the screen?
8   What does the cursor indicate on a word processor?
9   State two differences between a dot matrix printer and a daisy wheel printer.
10   Why is it advisable to compile your own operator's manual?

PART II
TEXT EDITING I

Chapter 2

Text Editing and Initial Functions of Word Processing

2.1 Deleting

How deletion is achieved depends upon the machine used. On some machines a key will be marked Char Del. This will delete one character. Another key will be marked Line Del, and this will delete the whole line of the text from wherever the cursor is positioned to the last character on that line. Another key will be marked Para Del, which when pressed will delete the whole of the paragraph. If any of these deletion keys is pressed twice then two words, lines or paragraphs will be deleted.

The word, line or portion of text to be deleted is usually highlighted on the screen before it is deleted thereby giving the operator the chance to cancel the command if the incorrect portion of text has been indicated.

Some machines give the option of deleting the character immediately to the left and right of the cursor position, by using a key marked Del← or Del→. Another option given on some machines is that of marking the beginning of the text to be deleted and pressing a 'cut' key followed by the cursor which will shade in and highlight the areas covered by the cursor movement; then, by pressing the execute key all the highlighted text is removed. The text following the deletion, will be moved up automatically to close any gaps which would be left.

Exercise 2A Deleting characters, including carriage returns

Using a margin of 1″ either side type the following passage. Do not erase the screen when the exercise is completed but turn to the next page for further instructions.

Do not press the carriage return key at the end of each line, but press this twice when a new paragraph is required. You will notice the symbol to show this on the screen which may look like ◁ or ↵.

The new word processing operator should notice the key marked 'delete'. This key is used to delete letters or characters. A carriage return is treated as a character and if this needs to be deleted the cursor is positioned over it and the deletion key is pressed.

The same characters could be deleted by using either the backspace key or the spacer bar. These bad habits should be avoided and use the correct key used. Practise deleting a letter 'i' first.

Exercise 2B Deleting characters, including carriage returns

Delete the characters which are indicated by a line struck through them and the ♏ sign appearing in the margin on the same line as the word which is to be deleted.

♏ The new word processing operator should notice the key marked 'delete'. This
key is used to delete letters or characters. A carriage return is treated as
a character and if this needs to be deleted the cursor is positioned over it
and the deletion key is pressed. ⌐

         RUN ON HERE – i.e. DELETE CARRIAGE RETURNS.

The same characters could be deleted by using either the backspace key or the
♏ space bar. These bad habits should be avoided and use the correct key used.
♏ Practise deleting a letter first.

Exercise 3A Deleting words

Using a margin of 1″ either side type the following passage.

    Do not erase the screen when the exercise is completed but turn to the next page for further instructions.

It was mentioned in the introduction to this book, that when a word or a carriage return is deleted, the word processor will automatically move up the text to close the gap left by the deleted text.

We should perhaps mention here that very often the key used to delete one character is different from the key used to delete several characters. Although the character deletion key can be pressed four times to remove the word 'word' this would be a waste of time, so if one key can be used to remove all four letters at once so much the better. The key we have just referred to is probably marked, Del. Word.

Exercise 3B Deleting words

Delete the words indicated.

It was mentioned in the introduction to this book, that when a word or a
carriage return is deleted, the word processor will automatically move ~~up~~ the
text to close the gap left by the deleted text.

We should perhaps mention ~~here~~ that ~~very~~ often the key used to delete one
character is different from the key used to delete several characters.
Although the character deletion key can be pressed four times to remove the
word '~~word~~' this would be a waste of time, so if one key can be used to
remove all four letters at once so much the better. The key we have just
referred to is ~~probably~~ marked, Del. Word.

Exercise 4A Deleting lines

Using a margin of 1″ either side type the following passage. Do not
erase the screen when the exercise is completed but turn to the next
page for further instructions.

Probably before purchasing your first word processor your
employer asked you to visit an exhibition where several word
processors were on display stands.

One is often held at Wembley and is the Which Word
Processor Exhibition.

Exhibitions serve to familiarise new would-be operators with
the appearance and style of the machines but at this stage
their knowledge is insufficient to be able to make a
judgement as to which machine they would prefer.

However, a friendly salesperson may give a good demonstration which is useful.

Exercise 4B Deleting lines

After proof-reading your work delete the lines which are struck through and indicated with 𝓗 a deletion sign in the margin.

Probably before purchasing your first word processor your employer asked you
to visit an exhibition where several word processors were on display stands.

𝓗   ~~One is often held at Wembley and is the Which Word Processor Exhibition.~~

Exhibitions serve to familiarise new would-be operators with the appearance
and style of the machines but at this stage their knowledge is insufficient
to be able to make a judgement as to which machine they would prefer.

𝓗   ~~However, a friendly salesperson may give a good demontration which is~~
~~useful.~~

Exercise 5A Deleting a paragraph

Using a margin of 1″ either side type the following passage. Do not erase the screen when the exercise is completed but turn to the next page for further instructions.

In the previous exercises a character, a word and a line have all been deleted.

It is also possible on a word processor to delete a paragraph in the middle of a piece of text or from the position of the cursor to the end of the typing in one operation.

This means that one paragraph can be completely removed from the section by one command, and the other paragraphs will move up.

How does the word processor know where a particular paragraph starts and ends? The start is marked by you positioning the cursor and the end is marked by the carriage return sign. On some systems it is necessary for you to mark the end of the paragraph with a symbol.

Exercise 5B Deleting a paragraph

Delete the first paragraph.

Delete the carriage return sign after the end of the new first paragraph, i.e. after the word 'operation'. This should now mean that the paragraph starting with the words 'This means that one paragraph . . .' etc. will join up to the first paragraph.

Exercise 6A Deleting the remaining text from the cursor point

Using a margin of 1″ either side type the following passage. Do not erase the screen when the exercise is completed but turn to the next page for further instructions.

A word processor as well as deleting text can also insert words and paragraphs into the middle of work which has already been typed.

This is a facility which is dearly loved by authors who have forgotten to mention a point in their report, and whereas typists used to have to retype the whole page before the advent of word processors, they can now simply slip in the forgotten paragraph.

Although this facility is a big help to the operator, and the author, one cannot help thinking that authors may be even less careful in preparing manuscripts than they were previously, simply because it is so easy to make insertions of extra material when the work is prepared on a word processor.

This fact can be shown by the number of times an author sends back the script to have pieces inserted. This means it takes a longer time to produce the final report.

**Exercise 6B Deleting the remaining text from the cursor
point**

The last two paragraphs are now considered unnecessary. Therefore
delete the last two paragraphs of this text, starting with the word
'Although'.

Your work should read as follows:

A word processor as well as deleting text can also insert words
and paragraphs into the middle of work which has already
been typed.

This is a facility which is dearly loved by authors who have
forgotten to mention a point in their report, and whereas
typists used to have to retype the whole page before the
advent of word processors, they can now simply slip in the
forgotten paragraph.

2.2 Inserting

Exercise 7A Inserting words

Using a margin of 1″ either side type the following passage. Do not erase the screen when the exercise is completed but turn to the next page for further instructions.

On most word processing systems it is an easy matter to insert. Most machines simply require that you go into insert mode by pressing the Insert Key or a Code Key and the I Key, for insert, and the piece to be inserted will be typed in at that point. However, on some machines, when in insert mode it is not possible to use the cursor to advance forwards and backwards and this can only be done by using the backspace key or the space bar. Other machines allow you to insert as much text as you want and then require that you reformat the text.

This means that you give an instruction to make the text fall into line with the rest of the typing on the screen, i.e. when in insert mode it will type outside the margins and you later tell it to line up the inserted text with the rest of the text on the screen.

When the machine is in insert mode it does not allow the operator to overtype a character. Therefore some systems allow the operator to switch off the insert facility and switch it on only when insertions are required. This can be useful—because it is sometimes necessary to merely change a small letter to a capital letter or to go back and underline or to change single inverted commas to double. However, if the machine is continually in insert mode then these operations require that a deletion followed by an insertion is made.

Exercise 7B   Inserting words

Insert the words and phrases shown below, where indicated.

On most word processing systems it is an easy matter to insert. Most
machines simply require that you go into insert mode by pressing the Insert
Key or a Code Key and the I Key, for insert, and the piece to be inserted
will be typed in at that point. However, on some machines, when in insert
mode it is not possible to use the cursor to advance forwards and backwards
and this can only be done by using the backspace key or the space bar. Other
machines allow you to insert as much text as you want and then require that
you reformat the text.

This means that you give an instruction to make the text fall into line with
the rest of the typing on the screen, i.e. when in insert mode it will type
outside the margins and you later tell it to line up the inserted text with
the rest of the text on the screen.

When the machine is in insert mode it does not allow the operator to overtype
a character. Therefore some systems allow the operator to switch off the
insert facility and switch it on only when insertions are required. This can
be useful because it is sometimes necessary to merely change a small letter
to a capital letter or to go back and underline or to change single inverted
commas to double. However, if the machine is continually in insert mode then
these operations require that a deletion followed by an insertion is made.

Exercise 8A Inserting, including inserting new paragraphs

Using a margin of 1″ either side type the following passage. Do not erase the screen when the exercise is completed but turn to the next page for further instructions.

What organisations would benefit from installing some kind of word processing equipment?

All organisations large and small can benefit from installing W.P. equipment, unless of course the staff within the organisation are unwilling to spend the time learning how to use the machine to its advantage. If they are unwilling then it will take longer to learn. Conflict may be caused and this leads to unhappiness of workers. There are various ways of overcoming conflict or 'resistance to change'; these include management techniques which pay attention to motivating the workers by awarding them a pay rise, or involving them in the decision as to which machine should be bought.

Exercise 8B Inserting, including inserting new paragraphs

Insert the words and phrases and the new paragraph where indicated.
Insert the new paragraph by positioning the cursor over the first letter
of the new paragraph and then pressing the carriage return key twice.

What organisations would benefit from installing some kind of word processing

equipment?

All organisations large and small can benefit from installing W.P. ✓in full

equipment, unless of course the staff within the organisation are unwilling

to spend the time learning how to use the machine to its advantage. [If they staff

are unwilling then it will take longer to learn.   Conflict may be caused and to learn them

this leads to unhappiness of workers.   [There are various ways of overcoming

conflict or 'resistance to change'; these include management techniques

which pay attention to motivating the workers by awarding them a pay rise, or

involving them in the decision as to which machine should be bought.

Exercise 9A Inserting and deleting

Using a margin of 1″ either side, type the following passage. Do not
erase the screen when the exercise is completed but turn to the next
page for further instructions.

Tomorrow's executive may not realise that his present
enthusiasm for the latest office toys could bring him to a
status where do-it-yourself paperwork is accepted as a matter
of course. At present the possession of new toys (office
technology) can give an impression of forward thinking and
innovative management—tomorrow they will become the
conveniences of automated clerical functions.

At present in most offices it is necessary for the manager to
have a person to do these chores for him—that person being
his personal assistant or secretary with all the attributes and
involvements of human relations. The personal assistant
plays the role of personal secretary, right-hand man/woman,
man/woman Friday, or respected slave who obeys the buzz
from an intercom with as much obedience as the butler used
to obey the call from the drawing room.

Exercise 9B Inserting and deleting

Insert and delete the words and phrases indicated.

The executive of

1.c. Tomorrow's ~~executive~~ may not realise that his present enthusiasm for the
latest office toys could bring him to a status where do-it-yourself paperwork
is accepted as a matter of course.   At present the possession of new toys
(office technology) can give an impression of forward thinking and innovative

these toys or tools

management – tomorrow ~~they~~ will become the conveniences of automated clerical
functions.

At present ~~in most offices~~ it is necessary for the manager to have a person
to do these chores for him – that person being his personal assistant or

n.P. secretary with all the attributes and involvements of human relations. The
ranging from surrogate wife/husband
personal assistant plays the role ~~of personal secretary, right-hand~~

to

~~man/woman, man/woman Friday, or~~ respected slave who obeys the buzz from an
intercom with as much obedience as the butler used to obey the call from the
drawing room.

2.3 Printing

In the introduction to this book it was mentioned that one of the
biggest barriers to learners of word processing was that of actually
switching on the machine and booting up the system. The next largest
barrier in my opinion is that of printing out the material, the achieve-
ment of the *hard* copy from the screen image, which is often known as
the *soft* copy. There is nothing so tangible as the first piece of paper
clutched in the hand of the new operator as proof of operation.

This piece of paper may soon become a relic of another age if
electronic mail and viewdata communication develop more rapidly.
Even today when many word processing operators do not see their
work actually printed out, because the printer is in a different room, it
is recognised that many operators will want to see their work and
provision is made for them to collect the printed sheets.

Why the barrier then if the psychological rewards are to see the work
in print? This stems from several sources.

(a) On some systems the layout on the screen is not the same as
that which is printed out.

(b) The paper needs to be positioned correctly in the printer and this is further complicated by the many physical attachments which can be added to the printer, such as continuous stationery feeding devices, sheet feeders which jog down one sheet after another at the press of a switch, or the acoustic hood which covers the printer in order to lessen the noise.

(c) Given that the paper guide, which denotes where the edge of the paper is positioned, is not always logically set at '0', the operator finds it difficult to comprehend the margin settings on the screen in relation to the position of the edge of the paper. This is especially difficult for the new operator if 'space' has to be allowed for the sprocket holes which appear down the edges of continuous stationery.

(d) The margin to be left at the top of the paper is sometimes determined by the number of carriage returns which the operator will have inserted on the screen before beginning to type. Alternatively the printer may be programmed to turn up a set number of lines from the top once the printer command has been given.

(e) The print menu can offer the choice of bold type, italic type, proportional spacing, over-striking or merely draft printing.

(f) There is the option of repeat printing, whereby one page of text can be printed several times, or the printing of a text, which means the first page of the document is printed and then a further command is given to print the second and subsequent pages.

(g) Some systems require that the operator exits from the word processing program before the printing command can be accepted.

(h) Other systems require the operator to make a choice to amend and print or print and abandon the document.

(i) Finally there is often a choice of printing directly from screen or printing from disk.

At this point we will assume that it is possible to print directly from the screen. Operators will need to refer to the manual regarding the positioning of the paper in the printer and the actual printer settings since these will vary with each system and are beyond the capacity of this book.

It is the intention here only to draw the reader's attention to the various options and at this point to concentrate principally upon printing directly from the screen, or if this is not possible, printing from disk.

Exercise 10 Printing

Using the preset margins type the following and then after proof reading your work, print the document. Remember to check the operator's manual for instructions before attempting to print.

There are several types of printers available which vary in speed of operation and the quality of the finished product. The most commonly used printers at present for word processing are daisy wheel printers. The hard copy produced by using a daisy wheel printer is of a high quality and gives the appearance of a printed or typewritten finish.

The daisy wheel, as the name implies, is a plastic wheel with petals forming the letters and the style of the letters produced can be changed by simply changing the wheel. The styles of print available range from standard type to ornate roman handwritten styles.

Daisy wheel printers are more expensive than dot matrix printers. Daisy wheels also operate somewhat more slowly than dot matrix printers, even though the wheel operates bi-directionally, that is once the printer head has reached the right hand margin by printing from left to right it then reverses and prints from right to left, so therefore no time is wasted in the printer head returning each time to the left margin. However, if the text is justified some printers do not perform bi-directional printing.

One of the latest types of printer used in word processing which gives a quality finish is the laser printer. In appearance these resemble a photo-copying machine and operate at high speeds. However, at present they are considerably more expensive than either dot matrix or daisy wheel printers.

2.4 Protected Spaces

Whilst typing the previous exercises it may have occurred to the operator that because of the automatic wraparound facility the machine splits up words which preferably the operator would position on the same line. This can be avoided by the operator using protected spaces.

Protected spaces are spaces in which the operator has inserted a code. The code is often achieved by pressing a function key or the code key at the same time as the space bar is pressed. This is indicated on the screen by a small symbol which looks like □ or △. The reason for using this is, as the name implies, to protect that space, that is it ensures that two or more words always remain on the same line as each other, if the spaces between them are protected. This is necessary when typing names or proper nouns. The wraparound facility on the word processor sometimes means that a forename can appear at the end of one line and the corresponding surname at the beginning of the next. In conventional printing, it is generally accepted that names and dates are not split up.

The most common mistake an operator makes here is to type the first name, i.e. 'Shahid', insert a protected space, then type another space before typing the surname, 'Patel'. The machine does not keep the two names together because one of these spaces has not been protected, but it is easy for the operator, unaware of the extra space she has inserted, to assume that the machine is not obeying this coded instruction.

Remember to use protected spaces every time a group of proper nouns is typed, even though these may not appear to be near to the end of the line of type; after insertions or deletions they very well could be placed at the end of the line. Also remember to protect the spaces inserted on either side of a dash, because a line beginning with a dash is not acceptable in conventional printing.

Exercise 11 Protected spaces

Type the following exercise using a 2″ margin on both sides, and a pitch of 12 spaces to 1″.

First do not use protected spaces between the proper nouns and watch how the machine will split these up using the wraparound facility.

The Head of this Organisation is called Mr. D. J. Bottomley.

The Managing Director's name is Mr. Michael David Smith.

Many tourists enjoy visits to the Changing of the Guard at Buckingham Palace.

Now retype the same sentences, this time using protected spaces.

Do not assume that you can go back and insert protected spaces without retyping part of the phrase. Some systems although appearing to accept the code by placing the symbol on the screen, will not obey it if the words on either side of the protected spaces are not retyped.

> The Head of this Organisation is called
> Mr. D. J. Bottomley.
>
> The Managing Director's name is
> Mr. Michael David Smith.
>
> Many tourists enjoy visits to the
> Changing of the Guard, at Buckingham Palace.

2.5 Justification

Used in word processing or typewriting, the term 'justification' refers to the right-hand margin requiring a straight edge.

Because words vary in length some will end before reaching the right-hand margin setting. This gives the appearance of a ragged text. When typing the last word immediately before the right hand margin setting, the machine will count the number of letters and if this exceeds the number of spaces left on that particular line of type, the machine will wraparound the whole word to the next line, leaving a few blank spaces before the right-hand margin on the previous line. This gives the appearance of a ragged edge.

Such a ragged edge is perfectly acceptable in business letters and memos, but, some documents, including reports, are often presented in such a way as to look as though they have been printed. Therefore, they need a justified right-hand margin.

On most word processors a command is given to justify or straighten the text followed by the identification of the amount, i.e. the whole page, one paragraph, or half a page. What the machine does is to space out the words, so that any blank spaces which would normally be left before the right-hand margin, are taken up between each of the words and the effect is not noticeable to the reader.

When the command to justify is given to the machine, it is sometimes evident from the screen, that this command has been given, because the right-hand margin looks even. However, on some machines the command is accepted by symbols appearing on the screen—sometimes at the left margin, which may confuse the operator, because the left margin is in fact always justified since all words begin at the same point. On other systems, the justification is a preset condition within the program whereby everything that is typed is automatically justified.

An intermediate choice is also available on some systems whereby the text can be semi-justified. This means that whereas a ragged margin may leave seven or eight spaces at the end of a line, a semi-justified margin will ensure that only three or four spaces are left.

On systems where the incremental spaces between the words are used, the operator must remember to include a carriage return at the end of every short line, otherwise it will space out the words so that a simple sentence of five or six words could extend right across the page. For example:

We   thank   you   for   your   help.

This looks peculiar and should be avoided.

Exercise 12A Justification of entire document

Using a margin of 1″ on either side, type the following passage. Do not erase the screen when the exercise is completed but turn to the next page for further instructions.

COMPUTERS AND FILING

A word processor or computer can often be invaluable in selecting certain records from a file and it can do this without disturbing the original file. Imagine going through a filing cabinet drawer (or a card index box) taking out several folders or records from different places. It would be necessary to replace the folders with 'out' cards showing where the folder had gone to. The 'out' card would also denote to the filing clerk, where to re-file the record. However, imagine a clerk's frustration upon going to the filing cabinet only to find that the folder he urgently requires has been borrowed by someone in another department. It is at this point that he will demand a departmentalised filing system, where each department has their own files and if one folder is needed by two different departments all the contents are copied and each keep their own folders/records.

When computerised filing is used it means that the same centralised filing system can be used by every department at the same time, so long as all the terminals are inter-connected to the central computer. Instead of a record or folder being taken out of the main system the information within it can be withdrawn for viewing on a VDU on the clerk's own desk, and if another clerk should require to use this same record at that very moment they too can recall it to their own VDU and work upon it also.

Exercise 12B Justification of entire document

After proof-reading your work delete the lines which are struck through and indicated with the delete sign in the margin and insert the words and phrases shown where the insert sign appears.
   Justify the right-hand margin.
   Print the document.

COMPUTERS AND FILING

A word processor or computer can often be invaluable in selecting certain
records from a file and it can do this without disturbing the original file.
Imagine going through a filing cabinet drawer (or a card index box) taking

out several folders or records from different places. It would be necessary

to replace the folders with 'out' cards showing where the folder had gone to.

The 'out' card would also denote to the filing clerk where to re-file the

record. However, imagine a clerk's frustration upon going to the filing

cabinet only to find that the folder he urgently requires has been borrowed

by someone in another department. It is at this point that he will demand a

departmentalised filing system, where each department has their own files and

if one folder is needed by two different departments all the contents are

copied and each keep their own folders/records.

When computerised filing is used it means that the same centralised filing

system can be used by every department at the same time, so long as all the

terminals are inter-connected to the central computer.   Instead of a record

or folder being taken out of the main system the information within it can be

withdrawn for viewing on a VDU on the clerk's own desk, and if another clerk

should require to use this same record at that very moment they too can

recall it to their own VDU and work upon it also.

Exercise 13A Justification

Using margins of your own choice type the following passage and justify the first three paragraphs only. Print from screen, but do not erase the screen.

Home shopping is becoming one of Britain's biggest growth areas open to traditional retailers.

Although there are several social reasons for this, the logistics of organising the paper-work, record keeping and complicated distribution procedures which accompany home shopping, have been considerably reduced by the use of word processors and computerised record keeping.

The following are some of the advantages which such technology offers to this form of retailing.

A computerised sales organisation, which gives exact information about the customers.

Exact information about the customers on record.

It encourages sales from more non-High Street shoppers.

Customers can use television for computer ordering of goods.

It reduces the need for retailers to acquire more High Street space.

If written communication is needed the facility of word processors to merge standard letters with different variables makes this communication easy.

Exercise 13B Erasing the justification

Carry out the corrections shown and erase the justification.

Home shopping is becoming one of Britain's biggest growth areas open to

traditional retailers.

Although there are several social reasons for this, *growth* the logistics of

organising the *vast amount of* paper-work, *and* record keeping and complicated distribution

procedures which accompany home shopping, have been considerably reduced by

the use of word processors and computerised record keeping.

The following are some of the advantages which such technology offers to this

form of retailing.

~~A computerised sales organisation, which gives exact information about the~~

~~customers.~~

Exact information about the customers on record, *i.e. the most popular sizes requested, the price ranges bought, and socio-economic classification of the customer.*

It encourages sales from more non-High Street shoppers, *usually more affluent professionals who do not have the time to do traditional shopping.*
Customers can use television for computer ordering of goods.

It reduces the need for retailers to acquire more High Street space, *which is becoming more scarce and more expensive.*

If written communication is needed the facility of word processors to merge

standard letters with different variables makes this communication easy.

2.6 Hyphenation

Once margins are set on a word processor, the machine will use these to adjust the wraparound. On occasions a large gap may be left at the right-hand margin, because the word which should have followed in sequence was too long for the space. This can be adjusted by instructing the machine to justify the right-hand margin, so that all lines end at the same point, giving a straight right-hand margin. However, another facility exists to give the operator the choice of making a more acceptable right-hand margin, and that is the use of hyphenation.

On some systems there is a hyphenation assist facility. This means a code key and a function key are pressed, or the code key and the hyphen key, and the machine highlights those words which it can reasonably split to make the margin look neater, but not justified. The operator then has the choice of scrolling backwards or forwards within the highlighting to hyphenate the words at the most appropriate place, i.e. before a suffix or after a prefix.

Compound words which have a hyphen in them will remain hyphenated no matter where they appear on the line and the machine treats these as one word. Such compound words are 'money-box', 'above-mentioned'. These types of hyphens are known as 'hard' hyphens.

The term 'soft hyphen', used in word processing, means a code inserted into a word at a point where you would be happy for it to be split if it should come at the end of a line. An example is the word 'accommodation'. This may have a soft hyphen inserted as follows, 'accommoda-tion'. Unless the word does appear with one half on one line and the other half on the next line down, it would not require a hyphen and would constitute a spelling error. What a soft hyphen does therefore is to accept the operator's preference as to where the word should be split if it were to appear at the end of a line. If, after all the insertions and deletions to the text, it appears in the middle of the line, the machine will ignore this code and spell the word without the hyphen.

Exercise 14A Hyphenation

Using margins of your own choice, type the following passage, using any hard hyphens you consider necessary, and print from screen. Do not erase the screen but turn to the next page for further instructions.

In word processing we are concerned with the use of the hyphen to make the right-hand margin appear more even than it may do otherwise if the automatic wraparound facility is used. In the use of the English Language, however, there is much confusion regarding the use of the hyphen, and like all aspects of language, the trends and fashions change over time.

Some time ago it was not unusual to find the word today hyphenated, whereas it is commonly accepted as all one word. Also, whilst hyphens were frequently used to separate numbers printed out in words, e.g. twenty-two, thirty-six etc. many numbers are now typed as numbers.

The use of the hyphen, however, is still necessary in some words where prefixes or suffixes are used to form a new word. Examples of such words are 'self-contained', 'anti-freeze', 'self-defence' or adjectives such as the 'vertical take-off jump jet'.

Consider the following words and decide where you would insert a hyphen if necessary.

prepare, vacation, magnitude, magnanimous, transportation, significance, backward, thoughtlessness, membership.

Exercise 14B Hyphenation

Carry out the corrections as shown and using the hyphenation assist facility insert any soft hyphens you consider necessary before printing from screen.

In word processing we ~~are concerned with the~~ use ~~of~~ the hyphen to make the

right-hand margin appear more even than it may do ~~otherwise~~ if the automatic

wraparound facility is used.   In the use of the English Language, however, *l.c.*

there is much confusion regarding the use of the hyphen, and like all aspects

of language, the trends and fashions change over time.

Some time ago it was not unusual to find the word today hyphenated, whereas

it is *now* commonly accepted as all one word.   Also, whilst hyphens were

frequently used to separate numbers printed out in words, e.g. twenty-two,

thirty-six, etc., many numbers are now typed as ~~numbers~~ *figures, and the need*

does not arise

~~The use of the~~ hyphen, however, ~~is~~ *are* still necessary in some words where

prefixes or suffixes are used to form a new word.   Examples of such words are

'self-contained', 'anti-freeze', 'self-defence', ~~or adjectives such as the~~

'vertical take-off jump jet'.

Consider the following words and decide where you would insert a *soft* hyphen if

necessary. *operator*

Insert soft hyphens in these words

prepare, vacation, magnitude, magnanimous, transportation, significance,

backward, thoughtlessness, membership.

2.7 Centring

The word processor will centre any line or group of lines between two reference points, the left and right-hand margins. A whole block of text can be centred, but this function is used most frequently for headings.

The cursor is positioned on the first character of the line to be centred, a function key is pressed, and the option is then offered to the operator—sometimes by a menu—to select the amount to be centred, e.g. line, paragraph, remainder, etc. After the selection has been made the execute key is pressed and the text is centred.

If a deletion or insertion is later made to a centred heading, this means that a number of letters have been added to or deleted from that line, so therefore the heading is no longer centred and the machine will automatically return the typescript to the left hand margin and the operator has to carry out the command again.

The centring referred to here is horizontal centring only. Some dedicated word processors will actually centre text vertically as well. This can be used for documents which need to be displayed, such as menus or agendas.

The material is typed with the appropriate line spacing separating the items or courses in the case of a menu, and then the cursor is positioned on the first letter of the text. The machine will centre the lines of typescript and the spaces between them within the preset page length. The page length for an A4 sheet is usually set at 54 or 56 lines on a word processor although this can be increased by the operator.

Exercise 15 Centring

Using A4 paper type and centre each of the lines below.
    Remember it may be necessary to bring down the ruler line to check the margins before giving the centring instruction.
    Print from screen.

Word Processing

Computing

The Electronic Office

Local Area Network

Viewdata

Prestel

Exercise 16 Centring

Using A5 paper type and centre each of the lines below.
    Remember it may be necessary to bring down the ruler line to check the margins before giving the centring instruction.

(a) your own name

(b) your nationality

(c) your date of birth

(d) your home town

(e) the name of your school or college

Exercise 17 Centring

Type the following menu, centring each line of text.

Notice that the menu is one often found in word processing. It enables the operator to position the cursor over a particular point and then execute the command. Such a menu can be used on some machines when changing the pitch.

Character Spacing

10 pitch

12 pitch

15 pitch

Line Spacing

single spacing

double spacing

treble spacing

Layout

new layout

edit layout

Typing Styles

Bold Type

Italic Type

Proportional Type

Exercise 18 Centring

Using A4 paper, type the following advertisement.

Centre the longest line of the text and then block all other lines to this so that the advertisement appears as a small block centred in the middle of the page, horizontally.

Word Processing Operator required to join a team of operators in an expanding Company. The salary is terrific but your word processing skills must match it. It is important that applicants are familiar with at least two systems of word processing and preferably have experience of using an integrated system for information searches and communication as well as purely word processing.

If you feel that you can cope with the demands of tomorrow's office today, send us your CV typewritten please, but enclose a covering hand-written letter stating why you feel you are suitable for this Post.

Applications to be received before the last day of this month, and sent to:

Karen Cuncliffe, Transparent Office Systems Ltd,
York House, Sunrise Gardens, Manchester M10 1AA.

2.8 Upper Case Mode/Capitalisation

A facility which is often available on a word processor is that of using capital letters without engaging the shift lock key (on some keyboards there is a caps lock key in addition to a shift lock key). This enables the operator to type the letters A-Z in upper case and also the numbers 1-9. This is particularly useful when the operator is using numbers and capital letters simultaneously. Without this facility it is necessary to remember to remove the shift lock every time a number has to be typed, because on a qwerty keyboard numbers are typed with the machine in lower case.

A visual indication is often given to the operator on the status line to remind them that the machine is in 'upper case mode' and this may be shown by a symbol such as U or CAPS.

Exercise 19 Upper case mode/capitalisation

Using A5 paper type the following itinerary using the upper case mode or capitalisation facility on the machine.

0900	DEPART MANCHESTER PICCADILLY
1230	ARRIVE LONDON EUSTON
1315	BUFFET LUNCH–HEAD OFFICE
1400	CONFERENCE BEGINS
1700	CONFERENCE ENDS
1800	DEPART LONDON EUSTON
2130	ARRIVE MANCHESTER PICCADILLY

2.9 Automatic Underlining

The automatic underlining facility allows the operator to select a particular mode of operation whereby everything which is typed whilst the machine is in this mode will appear as underlined both on the screen and on the hard copy. This is a time saving and useful function particularly when headings are used which consist of two or three lines which all need to be underlined, e.g. in the heading preceding Minutes of Meetings:—

VIEWDATA INTERNATIONAL SUPPLIES LTD.

MINUTES OF ANNUAL GENERAL MEETING

Held at

The Head Office of the Company

Princes Street

Edinburgh

Scotland

Great Britain

on

Thursday 26th July 19——

A visual indication to the operator that the machine is in this mode of operation is given on the status line which shows a small line, i.e.—. However, on some systems, automatic underlining is a special print function, and it requires the selection from a style or emphasis menu in order to enact the print command. The option is often available to underline the words only and leave the spaces free, or alternatively full underlining can be selected and the complete line of type is underlined including all spaces between the words.

On some systems it is necessary to insert a particular control command whereby symbols are placed at the beginning and at the end of the text to be underlined. Only the symbols appear on the screen, but when the document is printed out the line of text is underlined. These symbols consist of a letter, which can make proofreading difficult because the operator reads the letter as part of the first word. It is possible to 'hide' all printer controls, which means that the symbol does not appear on the screen, but the operator must remember that this command has been given. In some instances a plus sign is placed at the beginning of the line to be underlined and a minus sign placed at the end of it.

If after typing a piece of text which has been underlined, it becomes necessary to erase the underlining then it is possible to give the machine a command to remove the underlining only and leave the rest of the text intact.

Like many operations on a word processor, the same function keys which are used to set the mode of operation are also used to cancel it, i.e. the plus sign changes to a minus sign and the reverse command is executed, or the underline key is again pressed to cancel the command.

Exercise 20A Automatic underlining

Using the automatic underlining facility, type the following. Centre and underline each line then print from screen. Do not erase the screen.

VIEWDATA INTERNATIONAL SUPPLIES LTD.

MINUTES OF ORDINARY GENERAL MEETING

Held at

The Regional Office of the Company

The Strand

Douglas

Isle of Man

on

Friday 29th August 19--

Exercise 20B Removal of underlining

Now erase the underlining only and print again from screen.

Exercise 21 Automatic underlining

Using margins of 1″ either side type the following passage. Remember to use the automatic underlining key if this is available, or insert the special print commands to achieve this.

Print from screen.

FIRST DAY AT THE OFFICE

It was Julie's first day at the Office. Her first day at work in fact. She was shown to her <u>work-station</u> by the Supervisor, Jean, who carefully explained to her about the net-working system, pointing out that although the central computer was a <u>multi-user system</u>, each of the <u>stand-alones</u> was independent, yet linked—giving access to a common core of disk space and data stored on disk. Julie would be allocated a <u>workspace</u> and she could <u>access</u> other people's <u>workspaces</u>—unless these had been designated as confidential, in which case only the person issued with a <u>password</u> could gain access to these. "So if you want to know the directors' salaries, you can't without knowing the password," she said cheerfully and then departed to the bubbling expresso coffee maker, which too was controlled by a micro chip, its <u>password</u> for coffee with cream being CC.

Julie felt totally bewildered and confused, because Jean had talked to her in terms with which Julie was completely unfamiliar, in other words in computer jargon.

Test Yourself

Having read the last few sections, you will have noticed that the passages all attempt to explain various aspects of word processing. As in most subjects, word processing and computing have their own language, or jargon.

From the passages it should be possible for you to ascertain the meaning of some of these words.

Try to answer the questions below, referring back to the passages you have read if necessary.

1 What is another word that in computer/word processing terms means the same as program?
2 What do you understand by 'booting up' the system?

3   What does the cursor show you on the screen?

4   What do you understand by the term wraparound?

5   What do the letters VDU stand for?

6   What do you understand by 'hard copy'?

7   What do you think peripherals are?

8   What does the status line show?

9   What does the format line show?

10   What is meant by the term 'justify the right-hand margin?

11   When are protected spaces used, and why are they used?

12   What is meant by 'hard hyphens'?

13   What is meant by 'soft hyphens'?

14   What is uppercase mode?

15   What advantage does the automatic underlining facility offer to the word processor operator?

16   When might an operator use proportional spacing?

17   In Exercise 21 certain terms were underlined.
      Try to explain these terms in your own words before checking your answers on page 58.

18   Whilst sitting in front of the machine but without consulting the operator's manual or your notes, or the menu on the word processor, write down the commands to carry out the following functions; remember to check your answers afterwards with your own personal manual.

Write the command:

   to set the left margin,

   to set the right margin,

   to centre a heading,

   to delete a character,

   to delete a line of text,

   to delete a carriage return,

   to use the hyphenation facility,

   to achieve a protected space,

   to justify a paragraph,

   to justify the whole passage.

Explanations of some of terms used in Exercise 21

Work-station
This is the console including the VDU and keyboard, it may also include the disk drive and the printer.

Multi-user system
A system whereby all work terminals are connected to one central CPU.

Stand-alones
A number of word processors or personal computers which each have their own CPU, keyboard, disk drive and printer, i.e. they are a complete unit.

Workspace(s)
This is the area of the disk which is allocated to a particular user.

Access
In computing terms this means to gain entry to the system and use that particular part of the disk.

Password
This is a code which is given to certain designated areas of the disk, so a person who does not know this word cannot hope to gain entry to that part of the disk. It is used for security of confidential documents.

PART III

DISK MANAGEMENT I

Chapter 3

Saving Documents on Disk

One of the biggest advantages of a word processor is the facility to save documents on to magnetic media, normally floppy disk or hard disk, from which the contents can be recalled to the screen and amendments incorporated without the need to retype the whole document.

A document can be saved by typing in a document name and pressing a key (normally a function key), which refers to the disk. The name chosen may be limited to a number of characters, or digits. As the disk drive reads the screen and writes the contents of this to the disk, a red light often appears on the disk drive. The document then remains on disk under that name until such time as it is deleted by the operator.

If it becomes necessary to amend this at a later date, then the document is recalled from disk to the screen, again by using a function key and typing in the name of the document or positioning the cursor over the name of the document as it appears on the index. Once on the screen, the deletions or insertions can be made. It is important to note here that the corrections are made only on the screen at this point and if they need to be recorded on to the disk, then the machine must be instructed to change the document on the disk. This is known as 'updating the document', that is you ask the machine to read the screen again and change the document which is already on disk. Until this is done the document will remain on disk in its original state.

The contents of a particular disk can be viewed by calling up the index which is usually arranged in alphabetical order of the name or number of the document. If a document contains several pages, each page retains the same name as the first page, followed by a number, so that a document called 'Quotation' will show the second page as 'Quotation.1', and the third page as 'Quotation.2' and so on. Multi-page documents are known as texts, on some systems, others merely treat a document as a document no matter how many pages it is in length.

3.1 Disk Management

Disk management is about managing the material put on disk and includes the following items:

   (i) the organisation of the files on the disk, including the naming of disks, pages and texts;

  (ii) deleting a disk, or deleting a page, or a text;

 (iii) inserting a page into an existing text;

 (iv) changing the name of an existing page or piece of text on disk;

  (v) duplicating a disk, or page of text.

Naming a disk

A disk may be given a name which will indicate the contents. This is especially useful if all the contents of the disk are of a similar nature, e.g. all quotations, then the disk may be named 'Quotations'. The choice of names or numbers of the pages and text will depend upon organisational choices and procedures, but each document should have a unique name or number for identification. Regarding the amount of space left free upon the disk, it is always advisable to leave some segments, so that if existing documents need additions made to them there is enough space left on the disk for this to be done.

Deleting a disk

Like all filing systems, documents are not kept for ever, so a word processing operator should spend some time deleting unwanted pages or cleaning entire disks ready for future use. Before doing so it is important to check that only the intended documents are deleted, otherwise this could mean a great deal of retyping. Any disks which contain standard formats which are used again and again, should have a protect sticker stuck over the notch in the disk, so that anyone who inadvertently tries to delete such a disk will find the machine gives an error message, thus warning the operator that for some reason the disk should not be deleted.

Inserting a page

Mention has been made of a multi-page document where the first page is saved under a particular name and subsequent pages, saved as part of that document, are automatically given the name of the original page. With reference to the aforementioned document 'Quotation', it may be that the word processing operator needs to type an additional page to that quotation, which needs to be inserted after page 1 and before page 2. In order to do this a page will need to be inserted. The way of doing this will vary from system to system, but it may be necessary to type the new page, calling it a relevant name, i.e. 'Quotation.1A' and then, so that the text follows on, instructing the machine to insert 'Quotation.1A' after 'Quotation.1'. Other systems may treat this as any insertion and automatically readjust the page numbering without the operator having to instruct the machine to do so.

Renaming a document

Names of documents can be changed, without affecting the contents, or even calling up the document in question to the screen. This keeps the index in order.

Duplicating a disk

All disks which contain standard letters, standard forms or master documents of any kind should have a back-up copy, kept separately from the disks which are in every day use. This is a security procedure, because it may have taken many hours to type in these standard forms. Similarly it may equally be necessary to take a back-up copy of a single page or a text, because these may contain important formulae which could be needed for future reference purposes, long after the original has been deleted. If the machine has a double disk drive, it is a simple matter to insert the disk to be copied into one of the drives and a blank disk into the other and instruct the machine to duplicate the contents. However, if the machine has only one disk drive then it becomes necessary to insert the disk which needs to be copied into the drive, call up to the screen the page to be copied, remove the disk, insert a blank disk and rememorise the page from the screen. If it is a full disk which is being copied this can take some considerable time. Machines with single disk drives are often cheaper than those with double disk drives, but if an organisation purchases two machines, then it is advisable that at least one of the machines should have a double disk drive.

3.2 Save, Recall, Update

You should first read the introduction to this chapter, then consult the summarised step by step guide below. At the same time try to perform these practically upon the machine. Remember to consult the operator's manual for your particular machine.

Saving

1   Ensure that the work disk is in the disk drive.
2   On some systems it is necessary that you tell the machine that you wish to create a new document, and give the document a name before typing it; on others the name is given after the document has been typed.
3   Type the document. For the purpose of this exercise, type only your own name and address, without the postal code.
4   Save this to disk—again some systems will require that you exit from the document and a menu will appear on the screen giving a choice of continue editing, save and continue, save and print, etc. The cursor is normally positioned over the option to be chosen and the execute key is pressed.

On such a system, if the cursor is positioned over the abandon edit line and the execute key is pressed then all the contents of the screen will disappear—never to return.

On other systems a code key followed by a function key are pressed in order to save a document. Again, check the menu and do not select the command which quits the current text without saving it.

Dedicated word processors merely require that the operator presses the function key for 'file' or 'disk' followed by M for memorise and then the name is typed in and the execute key pressed.

Whichever method is adopted you should now 'save' the document on disk.
5   Some systems will now return to the opening menu others will retain the text typed on screen—until the screen is cleared.

Recalling the document

1   You now decide to add the postal code to your name and address—so you need to recall the document.
2   To do this you have to select the command key for editing a document. After you have pressed this, the machine may ask for the name of the document. This has to be typed in or selected by means of positioning the cursor over the name of the document which appears in a list of names on the screen. Alternatively the file key is pressed and letter R for recall and the name typed in followed by the execute key. When you have given the command to recall or edit, the document should appear on the screen.

Updating the document

1 Add the postal code to your address.
2 Remember the postal code will only appear on the screen at this stage and therefore the document needs to be altered on disk. This is called 'updating' the document.
3 To do this may require the operator to exit and instruct the machine to finish editing–or alternatively the update key is pressed. Some systems actually flash the name of the document on the screen again at this command just to remind the operator which document is being updated and if this is the wrong one the cancel key can be pressed. Other systems offer the option to abandon edit and if this is selected the extra piece, i.e. the postal code, will be abandoned and the original document will remain on the disk. Some systems actually keep both versions of the document on the disk as a safeguard–naming the first one typed with the name, followed by the suffix, BAK. Once the up-date command has been given the document has been changed on the disk as well as on the screen.

3.3 Index/Directory

If the operator wishes to see the names of the documents on that particular disk then it is possible to call up the index or the directory and this should give a list of the names of the documents in alphabetical order.

The index is used by operators as any other index would be used to see which files are in that record:

1 to check that a document is on that particular disk prior to recalling it;
2 to use for disk management purposes (see section on disk management) i.e. when files are deleted from the disk;
3 to check there is available space left on that disk.

You should now practise calling up the index or the directory to your disk.

3.4 Some Questions

Text books, unlike novels, are not often read from beginning to end, because text books tend to be referred to randomly. However, if you have read the first few topics in this chapter you should by now know that all persons operating a word processor or a computer will have to apply different rules to their filing procedures. Instead of filing papers in a filing cabinet they now file documents electronically upon disk. Several questions spring to mind here; some of the more common questions are given below.

1   What about copies to Branch Offices?
2   Can you use carbon copies with the printer?
3   What about confidentiality?
4   How do you know what is on each disk?
5   What happens if a disk gets damaged, and the machine can not read it?
6   What happens if someone updates a document wrongly?
7   How do you dispose of old copies?
8   How long do you keep documents stored on disk?
9   How can you remember what you actually called a document?
10 How do you store the actual disks?

Try to answer these questions yourself from your own experience, before looking at the suggested answers below.

Suggested answers to questions on disk management

1   There are two solutions to this problem:
  (a) print out two copies of the document and post one as usual;
  (b) if your Branch Office has a word processor which is connected to the Head Office via a modem and telephone or by hard wiring, then send the script in the same way as you would send a telex message.
2   On some daisy wheel printers the answer to this questions is 'yes', but why do so when it takes only seconds to print out another original, or to produce a photocopy?
3   Regarding confidentiality—if we are concerned only with people actually reading the screen, whilst the document is being typed, then unless the potential 'mole' or 'inquisitive clerk' is as close to the screen as the operator, they would need very powerful spectacles or contact lenses to be able to read it. However, if the operator leaves the console whilst the document is on the screen, this in itself would be a breach of regulations in most companies and would not be allowed.

  Regarding an unauthorised user keying into confidential documents, if these reside on a hard disk, which could be used with a multi-user system, then each operator can be designated their own area and in order to access this area, will need to type in a password. The unauthorised user would not have the password, and if they should try to peer over the shoulder of the authorised user whilst they are typing in the password, they will be disappointed, because most systems take the precaution of not showing the letters of the password on the screen as the letters are typed in.

If the confidential documents are stored on floppy disk, then a simple precaution is to store these in a locked disk storage box and allocate an innocuous name or number to the 'hot' document which would not make it easy for the 'mole' to recognise the content of the document without calling it up to the screen.

4 When word processors are first introduced into offices, many operators using floppy disks print out the actual index of the disk and store this in the disk envelope. This makes a mockery of the paperless office of tomorrow, but there is always a grave temptation to do this, simply because it is in a form which can be read without inserting the disk into the machine.

5 If a disk is damaged and the machine can not read it, then unfortunately the operator has to retype the document if she has not taken a back-up copy. However, with attention given to the care of disks (see 10 below) this is preventable.

6 When someone updates a document some systems retain the original document adding the suffix .BAK. to its title in the index.

With floppy disks, it is possible to protect the disk from being updated by inserting a piece of silver paper over the notch in the disk, this prevents the machine from writing to the disk, but allows it to read the disk. If the operator tries to write to such a protected disk, the machine should give an error message and this will remind the operator that this disk should not be updated.

7 Depending upon the policy of the company, the clerk dictating a letter for later processing may be allowed to allocate the time period for which the document is to be stored on disk. This may vary from one week to one month to three months. Since some systems automatically type in the date and a code this can be typed in to denote which period of time has been chosen. It may be necessary from time to time to inspect the disks and erase all out of date documents. There are many different ways of organising this, but the key point to remember is each document should have a unique name and number and date for retrieval and later disposal.

8   Many of the aspects of this question have been covered above, but you should always remember that certain documents may be kept for a long period of time, e.g. standard letters inviting people for interview, or letters sent from a dentist informing patients of a repeat appointment for a dental check-up. All such standard documents may be kept until it is felt necessary to change the procedure. The completed letters will of course always be up to date because of the variables inserted.

9   The key point to remember is that each document should have a unique name or number, date and retrieval and disposal code. The actual names to be used often depend upon the organisation itself.

Consider your own organisation, even if this is your own school or college. Write down a list of all the different types of documents you may file on disk. Devise a system of naming these, which you consider suitable and give your reasons why.

10   It is important to store floppy disks in an upright position and each one should be inserted into the separate envelope provided. It is unwise to stack disks because they may become bent and this will corrupt the contents. Special disk storage boxes are available which have dividers for filing purposes and which can also be locked.

Hard disks are usually covered by a 'lid' when not in use on the machine.

3.5 Printing from Disk

Once the document has been saved on disk it is possible to give the command to print that named document directly from disk. What happens is that the print command is given, preceded or followed by the name of the document. The machine reads the document from disk and places its contents into a buffer memory. A buffer memory is a small piece of internal memory store which holds data prior to a further operation being performed upon it; the disk is then free to accept other commands. It is possible therefore, whilst the printer is printing one document, for the operator to be preparing another on the screen. This is known as concurrent printing.

Depending upon the printer used, the printer itself may have a buffer in it, which stores documents prior to printing. This extends the holding store for the documents whilst awaiting printing, so if two or more work stations are sharing one printer and both give the command to print at the same time, the printer will accept both and print out document number one but at the same time spool or queue document number two ready to print when document number one is completed.

In a large organisation there may be several printers serving many work stations. Because the printer format will vary according to the documents being prepared, i.e. some may need to be printed on A3 size paper, whilst others may require memorandum forms, the operator has to enact the command to direct the work to a particular printer which holds the appropriate paper. In other words, it is the printer code which directs the work.

Printers need resources and these include print wheels, and ribbons. If the hard copy is produced with one letter consistently omitted then the daisy wheel needs changing because one of the plastic petals has broken off—which happens after a heavy usage.

If the ribbon cartridge runs out, the printer stops abruptly, but an error message should be given on the VDU from which it received the work. The message may be coded, e.g. error message No. 5, and a check in the error manual will show a new ribbon must be inserted. Other systems merely print the error message 'resources'. After a new cartridge has been inserted it is possible to press the interrupt button and the printer will take up where it left off.

If the VDU has a function key known as stop/continue or interrupt then this may be pressed at any time whilst the printer is printing a document. The printer stops at the point where the key is pressed and remains there until the stop/continue key is pressed again; it will then continue printing. This function is different from the cancel print function key which stops the printer in the middle of printing a document. When the print continue key is pressed the printer will not continue from where it left off but rather return to the beginning of the document and start to print all over again.

Mention was made earlier of commands such as save and print, or the necessity to exit from the system before the print command is given. A reminder is made to the operator here that whilst the disk drive is reading the contents of the screen, i.e. saving it, prior to printing, it is quite possible that the lines of text on the screen will move rapidly, with a red light on the disk drive as the only indication that the contents are being read. If it is necessary to exit from the system, then the screen presents the opening menu, or in some instances presents a blank screen and the word processing program has to be re-accessed before the next document can be prepared. It is easy for the new operator at this stage to assume that they have lost the document, but within seconds the printer will begin to print it.

Whichever system is used a few common checks help to solve printing problems. These include:

(a) checking that the printer is switched on,
(b) checking that the printer has paper loaded in it,
(c) checking that the bail bar is in place,
(d) checking that the cover on the printer is closed,
(e) checking to see if a new ribbon is needed.

Without these checks the machine could give an error message and time will be wasted checking the error manuals, or worse still calling out the engineer.

3.6 Printer Accessories

Acoustic hood

An acoustic hood is literally a hood, usually with a transparent lid, which is placed over the printer in an attempt to lessen any noise which the printer makes. This is quite important if the printers are positioned in an open plan office where people are using telephones or speaking to clients and customers. It is also important from the office environment factor, since people are known to be affected by continuous noise, their concentration can be lessened if their surroundings are noisy and distracting.

Regarding convenience—some word processing operators are known to dislike the hoods because all have to be lifted or removed when the printer is loaded with paper and depending upon the design some need also to be lifted to remove completed letters.

Continuous paper feed/sheet feeders

It is impracticable for the word processing operator to have to load the printer with a sheet of paper every time a document is printed out. A continuous paper feed and sheet feeder are two devices which are a means of feeding the stationery into the printer continuously, without attention from the operator. The paper feed normally works on the principle that the paper has holes down each side which fit onto sprockets and the individual sheets have perforations which can be later separated.

The edges of the paper which contain the holes are removed or 'burst' by another machine before the printed letters are mailed. Sheet feeders simply hold a supply of separate sheets in a vertical position above the printer and these jog down one after the other as the machine is printing. The advantage of a sheet feeder is that the sheets do not have to be separated or burst after being printed. With this device it means that the word processing operator can give a print command to print continuously and the printer will print out page one followed by page two etc. without the need for a further command to be given. A repeat command can also be given whereby page one can be printed several times, simply by the operator typing R for repeat followed by the number of repeats required.

Exercise 22A Saving text

Type the following passage and save on disk. Call the document 'Procedures'. Erase the screen and turn to the next page for further instructions.

WORD PROCESSING UNIT

Every new operator will be given a supply of ten floppy disks. A locking disk storage box will also be supplied. Operators are reminded of the care of disks. This includes careful handling so as to avoid bending the disk. If disks do become bent this usually happens as they are inserted into the disk drive. It occurs quite accidentally but can be avoided by placing the disk gently into the drive before closing the door. Once the door has been closed a red light will indicate that the drive has registered the presence of the disk. If the red light does not come on then the operator should open the drive door and re-insert the disk.

Disks should be protected from dust and stored upright. The plastic boxes which are supplied in addition to the glass top disk storage boxes are primarily for temporary storage and are designed to hold ten 5¼" disks. On no account should more than ten disks be stored in these, otherwise as the box is closed there is a danger that the disks will be bent. On no account should disks be written on or their envelopes written on. This is the equivalent of applying a sharp pressure point and may corrupt the contents of the disk. Labels to indicate the contents of the disks should be prepared and later stuck onto the top of the disk.

Exercise 22B Resaving/updating text after editing, printing from disk

Recall the document called 'Procedures' and carry out the corrections shown.

Update the disk and print from disk.

WORD PROCESSING UNIT — CENTRE

Every new operator will be ~~given a supply of~~ ten floppy disks. A locking

disk storage box ~~will also be supplied~~. Operators are reminded of the care

of disks. This ~~includes~~ careful handling so as to avoid bending the disk.

If disks do become bent this usually happens as they are inserted into the

disk drive. It occurs quite accidentally but can be avoided by placing the

disk gently into the drive before closing the door. Once the door has been

closed a red light will indicate that the drive has registered the presence

of the disk. If the red light does not come on then the operator should open

the drive door and re-insert the disk.

Disks should be protected from dust and stored upright. The plastic boxes

which are supplied in addition to the glass top ~~disk~~ storage boxes are

primarily for temporary storage and are designed to hold ten 5¼" disks. On

no account should more than ten disks be stored in these, ~~otherwise as~~ the

box is closed there is a danger that the disks will be bent. ~~On no account~~

~~should~~ disks be written on, or their envelopes written on. This is the

equivalent of applying a sharp pressure point and may corrupt the contents of

the disk. Labels to indicate the contents of the disks should be prepared

and later stuck onto the the top of the disk.

3.7 Organisation of Disks

Index/directory

The index or directory of a disk is a list of all the items appearing on that disk and an example of a printed index page is given below:

	(a) SALES	(b) 40 Segments available
ACCOUNTS	MINUTES	REPORT
ACCOUNTS.1	MINUTES.1	REPORT.1
ACCOUNTS.2	MINUTES.2	REPORT.2
ACCOUNTS.3	MINUTES.3	REPORT.3
(c) AGENDA	(c) ORDER	REPORT.4
(c) LETTER	QUOTATION	
	QUOTATION.1	
	QUOTATION.2	

(a) This is the name given to the actual disk, by the operator.
(b) This shows how many segments are remaining on the disk and this figure is automatically reduced by the machine as more segments are used.
(c) A document which is only one page in length.

On some systems, the number of 'K' i.e. the number of characters, in thousands, used on each document is listed only: REPORT 32K, ORDER 7K. Obviously the longer the document the more characters will be used.

Notice also that on the example given the document names are listed in alphabetical order. Most systems do this automatically.

MARKETING 42 Segments available

AGENDA	REPORT.
FINANCE	REPORT.1
FINANCE.1	REPORT.2
FINANCE.2	REPORT.3
	REPORT.4
LETTER	REPORT.5

MINUTES

MINUTES.2

MINUTES.1

MINUTES.3

This example of the index of the same disk after some disk management tasks have been carried out shows:

   (i) the change of the name of disk from 'Sales' to 'Marketing';
  (ii) the change of the name of a text from 'Accounts' to 'Finance';
 (iii) the page document called 'Order' has been deleted from the disk;
 (iv) the text called 'Report' has had a page added to it;
  (v) the order of the pages within the text called 'Minutes' has been changed. Notice also how the number of segments have increased because some pages have been deleted.

Exercise 23 Correction of errors

Type the two pieces of manuscript, 'Hints to Travellers' and the letter addressed to Mr. J. Joseph.

Correct the spelling and punctuation errors which occur in these. After proof-reading the documents, save both documents on disk. Call the one entitled Hints to Travellers 'Hints'. Call the letter addressed to Mr. Joseph 'Letter'.

Print each document from disk.

HINTS. TO TRAVELLERS

Many people traveling on the trans-atlantic flights find that they suffer from jet-lag for the first two or three days after their arrival in the U.S.A.

Another name for jet lag could be lack of sleep, but generally it is a condition of maliase.

In order to minimise the effects of jet lag, after flying long distances, we would advise travelers to abstain from alcohol and drink regular quantities of water during the flight. This is to combat dehydration which is known to occur after four hours of flying.

DO'S & DONTS

DO NOT Smoke when the sign forbids you to do so.

DO NOT wear tight clothing.

DO drink plenty of non-alcoholic liquids.

DO eat lightly for the first few hours after landing.

Reproduced by kind permission of NWRAC Examinations Board. This passage is an adaptation of one which formed part of the NWRAC/ULCI Word Processing Grade II Examination, June 1985.

use today's date.

Mr. J. Joseph,
Travel Services Ltd.,
Southampton Road,
Bournemouth
BM3 1PD

Dear Sir,

In reply to your correspondance of yesterday requesting information for your clients who are visiting Florida, we now have pleasure in enclosing several brochures. However, we should like to point out that whilst the information is provided free of charge we do make a small charge for the stationary.
So that your clients may avoid any financial harassment, whilst on holiday, we would suggest they use there credit cards whenever possible, as this eliminates the problem of carrying a large ammount of cash.
Yours Faithfully,

Reproduced by kind permission of NWRAC Examinations Board. This passage is an adaptation of one which formed part of the NWRAC/ULCI Word Processing Grade II Examination, June 1986.

Exercise 24 Disk management, document delete and renaming documents

After consulting the operator's manual and the section on disk management, check how to delete a page from the disk and how to change the name of a document on disk.

Record the instructions in your personal manual in alphabetical order. It is suggested that the instructions for deleting items from disk are placed under the section on 'disk management'.

Call up the index or directory and if possible print this out.

Delete the page entitled 'Hints'.

Call up the index again to check this has now been deleted.

Change the name of the document entitled 'Letter' to 'Joseph', as this name is more meaningful than 'Letter' when the operator needs to recall it at some future date. The name 'Letter' could be a letter addressed to any number of people.

Print out a copy of the revised index/directory.

Exercise 25A Saving/updating/printing/document delete

Type the following and save on disk. Call the document 'Proof'. After saving it on disk, erase the screen.

PROOF READING

Proof-reading is reading and checking the words on the VDU screen before the text is printed out. This is important for two reasons, one of these being that the soft copy, once committed to be printed and converted into the hard copy, should be mailable, that is it should not contain any spelling, punctuation or layout errors, and secondly it may be the 'soft copy' which is actually mailed, i.e. electronically, so therefore it is equally as important that the completed work is accurate as it appears on the screen, before it is transmitted to another screen.

In order to proof read the operator must use the cursor to scroll both horizontally and vertically, and since the page width is often wider than the screen width, this technique of spotting errors sometimes takes time to learn.

Another drawback is that whilst scrolling it is easy to touch a key inadvertently and if this is the screen erase key or quit key, then the effect is serious since all the work typed is lost, therefore it is suggested that before proof reading the screen display, the work should be memorised and then if any errors are found these can be corrected and the file copy on disk updated.

Exercise 25B Saving/updating/printing/document delete

Check the index or directory to make sure the document named 'Proof' is listed. Recall the document and carry out the corrections shown. Update the document. Print from disk. After printing, delete the document from disk, and check the index to ensure that it has been erased.

PROOF-READING

Proof-reading is reading and checking the words on the VDU screen before the text is printed out. This is important for two reasons, one of these being that the soft copy, once committed to be printed and converted into the hard copy, should be mailable, that is it should not contain any spelling, punctuation or layout errors, and secondly it may be the 'soft copy' which is actually mailed, i.e. electronically, so therefore it is equally as important that the completed work is accurate as it appears on the screen, before it is transmitted to another screen.

In order to proof-read the operator must use the cursor to scroll both horizontally and vertically, and since the page width is often wider than the screen width, this technique of spotting errors sometimes takes time to learn.

Another drawback is that whilst scrolling it is easy to touch a key *inadvertently* inadvertently and if this is the ~~screen erase key or~~ quit key, then the effect is serious since all the work typed is lost, ~~therefore~~ it is suggested *u.c.* that before proof-reading the screen display, the work should be memorised *or saved* and then if any errors are found these can be corrected and the file copy on disk updated.

Chapter 4

Types of Disk

4.1 Floppy Disks

Disks vary in size as well as their physical form. There are 5¼″ and 8″ disks. These are known as 'floppy disks', as their magnetic medium is held in a thin flexible envelope. There are also 3½″ and 3″ disks which are somewhat more sturdy, because their magnetic medium is in a rigid plastic case.

The disk drives required to read these different disks will themselves vary in size and physical form and obviously the various sizes of disks will not be inter-changeable with the different types of disk drives.

The newcomer to word processing or computing may be excused for assuming that all 5¼″ disks will be interchangeable between different disk drives. However, as with most things, all is not what it seems. To begin with, the disk drives could be 'single-sided' which means that only one side of the floppy disk is used or 'double-sided' which means that both sides are used. Adding a further complication to this picture is the fact that different disk drives 'pack' their data on to the disk in various formats, some writing 40 tracks and others 80 tracks on to the disk. The density with which the data is written on to those tracks can also vary from disk drive to disk drive, so you can see that the transfer of work on disk, prepared on one machine but requiring to be used on another, is not as straightforward as it may appear.

Unless the two word processors or computers are the same model, or have the same operating system and disk format as each other, then it will not be possible to transfer work upon disk from one machine to another.

A few offices may be fortunate to have machines which are multi-format computers, in which the computer has different sizes of disk-drives allowing transfer of data between disks and work on any of the particular formats available. The obvious advantage of this facility is offset against the disadvantages of higher price which may not be justifiable for smaller businesses. One way around this transfer problem is to use the services of firms who will copy one format of disk to another. Costs vary depending upon what and how much needs to be copied but the expenditure could result in economy when set against the time saved.

Transfer of disks to another format may answer a question that might have occurred to you. What happens to all the records held on disk, should the company or firm change their machines?

4.2 Formatting Disks

Before a disk can be used, it has to be 'formatted'. This is a process which is carried out by the computer using a program within its operating system and what it does is to mark out concentric tracks round the disk and then divide these tracks into sections, the numbers of each of these depending on the system used. Having formatted the disk, the computer is able to write data on to this disk, since using the premarked settings it can calculate where to put the data and where to read it back. On other machines, and some dedicated word processors fall into this category, the operator has no way of formatting disks, so there is no choice but to buy the disks already formatted. This usually means buying them from the manufacturer of the hardware, in which case the prices are not as competitive.

4.3 Disk Capabilities

One aspect to consider when purchasing a machine, or planning disk management, is the capacity of the disks to hold data. Just as their sizes and formats vary, their capacity to store data also varies. However, manufacturers will quote disk capacities when giving the specification for their machines. These disk capacities could be quoted in the following way:

two disk drives, each of 400K capacity.

The important point here is the 400K. It stands for 400 kilobytes, a kilo being 1000 and a byte being a character, so that 400K=400 kilobytes or 400 000 characters. Not all this capacity can store word processing text, some of it is used by the computer for its own disk management.

The computer holds on disk a 'directory' of the text files that the operator has named and along with the file names, the sectors and tracks on which these files will be found. Depending on the system 2K may be taken up in this way leaving 398K for text storage. On an A4 page of 54 lines of type with a margin of 1″ either side, using a pitch of 12 characters to the inch, this works out at approximately 76 characters to the line and 54 lines each of 76 characters, which means that each page will contain approximately 4000 characters, using single line spacing. This would amount to 100 pages of text for each of the disk drives in the above example.

4.4 Winchester Disks

These disks may be known as rigid or hard disks as opposed to floppy disks, and the difference lies in their storage capacity which is so much greater than that of a floppy disk and also in the disk drive which houses such a disk.

Normally a Winchester disk drive will consist of a factory-sealed unit containing a solid disk coated with magnetic medium. This is capable of spinning at high speed. Above the surface of the disk is the read/write head which is positioned very close to the surface of the disk. However, when we use the term disk here we must think of it as a stack which consists of several flat circular metal disks, mounted together on a shaft, each disk being separated from the one above it by a few centimetres. The read and write heads are mounted in an arrangement like a comb and are able to access all the surfaces of the disks.

The Winchester disk has the capacity to store large quantities of data in the 10 megabyte to 40 megabyte range; more recently 140 megabytes have become available. As mega equals one million it is a small calculation to show that a 10 megabyte disk will store 10 million characters. Performing the same arithmetic as we did on the floppy disks, this means that it can store approximately 2500 pages of A4 text and with a 140 megabyte storage the capacity would be approximately 35 000 pages of A4.

Should your memory requirements be even greater there is the possibility of removable hard disk units with capacities of up to 70 megabytes. As you can imagine to have this type of capacity is an expensive purchase but lesser capacity Winchester disk drives are becoming cheaper as demand for them increases and more are produced.

Winchester disks may solve the problem of storage, but another problem is created because back-up copies of important data will need to be kept with one copy being safely stored in case of a mishap occurring with the original. This was mentioned in the section on floppy disks and it is still the case even with Winchester disks.

A way around the problem of back-up copies is to use floppy disks for important documents. However, the time it takes to do this and also the large number of floppy disks involved would be great. As an example, a computer with a 10 megabyte Winchester disk and a 360K 5¼" floppy disk drive would need 28 floppy disks to house a full Winchester disk. An alternative solution to the problem of back-up storage is to use an extra peripheral called a tape streamer. Some computers may have such a peripheral when purchased, but if not, one can be added to most standard equipment. In simple terms the tape streamer is like a large cassette tape which can quickly record the contents of the Winchester disk on to the tape. The capacity of the tapes is equivalent to a Winchester disk capacity of 20 megabytes. Obviously keeping control of one tape cassette is easier than keeping control of large numbers of floppy disks.

Unless the company is very small, with just one or two operators, some supervisory procedures should be set up to systematise the contents of the disks. For instance, all quotations may be stored on one floppy disk and these could be numbered with the month and the year; or if the firm deals with a lot of quotations, these may be arranged into alphabetical order of the names of the companies. One disk could be allocated to all potential customers with names beginning with A–L and another for potential customers with names beginning M–Z. Each quotation could be given the name of the company (or an abridged version of it) to whom it is addressed. Most word processors will file these automatically into alphabetical order on the disk.

On larger systems where a minicomputer is used each operator will be given an 'account number'. This will be the personalised reference number for each operator and will be followed by another code denoting the department. For example in a local authority the Planning Department will have the letter 'P' prefixed to every document and this will be followed by the date and the time when the document was typed and the number in ascending order of the number of documents produced by that department that month, or week. This code will be printed on to the document for reference purposes.

Test Yourself

The following questions concentrate upon the last few sections. Try to write the answers to them without consulting your notes. This set of questions relates to the practical operation of the machine, so it is suggested that you write down the function keys you would press on your machine in order to carry out the following. Remember to check your answers afterwards with your own personal manual.

How do you:

1　save a document on disk;
2　recall a document from disk;
3　update a document on disk;
4　call up the index or directory to the screen;
5　delete a page from the index;
6　change the name of a page on the disk;
7　print from disk;
8　delete a disk;
9　duplicate a disk;
10　name a disk?

The answers to the following questions are given on the next page.

11　What is the difference between a floppy disk which is single-sided and one which is double-sided?
12　Give another name for a daisy wheel?
13　What do you understand by disk management?
14　What checks should you carry out if the printer gives an error message?
15　What is a buffer?
16　What is the soft copy?
17　If the printer consistently omits to print one letter, what is the fault?
18　How can disks be protected from being updated?
19　When might it be necessary to duplicate a disk?
20　How can floppy disks easily become bent and as a result corrupt?

Suggested answers to questions 11-20

11   A floppy disk which is single-sided is one where data can be stored on one side only, whereas a double-sided disk is one where data can be stored on both sides. Therefore a double-sided disk holds much more data.

12   Another name for a daisy wheel is a print wheel. These are made of plastic and can be changed according to the style of type-face required, e.g. italics, or accented characters.

13   Disk management is the organisation of files on the disk i.e. deleting documents which are now obsolete, protecting files which should not be updated by using a protect sticker, naming disks and documents so that they are easily recognisable for recall and editing.

14   Checks to be made if the printer gives an error message include:
            check that it is switched on;
            check that there is paper in it;
            check that the cover is closed;
            check that no resources such as daisy wheels or ribbons are needed.

15   A buffer is an extra piece of memory which provides a temporary store prior to printing.

16   Soft copy is the screen copy.

17   If the printer consistently omits one letter the fault is in the daisy wheel. One letter or petal on the daisy wheel has probably fallen off owing to wear and tear. A new daisy wheel is required.

18   Disks can be protected from being updated by inserting a piece of silver paper over the notch so that the write head on the disk cannot operate.

19   It is necessary to duplicate a disk if it contains master copies of standard letters or forms which have taken many hours to record.

20   Floppy disks can become bent by careless insertion into the disk drive, or by storing them incorrectly, i.e. not in a properly designed disk storage box.

PART IV

TEXT EDITING II

Chapter 5

Tabulation, Reformatting, Moving Text

5.1 Tabulation Settings

Many word processing systems have preset tab stops positioned at intervals of five characters along the ruler/format line and these are indicated either by the letter T or some symbol such as a →.

These tabular positions are reached by the operator pressing the key marked 'Tab.' or the control key followed by a mnemonic code at which the cursor will jump to the first preset tab.

It is possible to clear the preset positions, however, and set new ones by positioning the cursor on the numerical horizontal position required and pressing the appropriate commands to set a tab. On some systems these settings will remain only whilst that document is typed, therefore if the ruler line with those particular tab settings is required again, then it must be 'saved'.

Other systems do not have preset tabs stops but allow the operator to position the cursor and set the tab whereby a letter T appears on the format/ruler line. This setting remains until it is cancelled by the operator.

In order to achieve a layout whereby the longest line in each column is equally positioned between the margins of that piece of work, the operator can use the centring function.

This is done by the operator setting equal margins and then typing in the longest line in each column with the appropriate number of spaces between the columns and then giving the command to centre the line. Once the centring has been carried out the tabs can be set above the first letter in each column thus denoting the position of the tab. The screen can then be erased and the format line is set up ready for the document in question.

It is possible to clear tabs by repositioning the cursor over the tab setting and pressing the same keys which were used to set it.

Alternatively the whole of the format/ruler line can be cleared by using one command which will erase all margins and tab settings.

Exercise 26 Tabulation

Type the following tabulation, using appropriate tabular stops.
   Print from screen.

3" Disks	Double Sided	Double Density
5¼" Disks	Double Sided	Single Density
8" Disks	Single Sided	Single Density
Disk Storage Boxes	Daisy Wheels	Multi-strike Ribbons
Reader Stands	Lighting Shields	Anti-glare Shield

Exercise 27 Tabulation

Type the following tabulation using either the preset tabular stops, but ensuring that at least five spaces are left after the longest line in each column before the commencement of the next one, or alternatively set appropriate tabular stops.
   Print from screen.
   Centre and underline the heading which should be typed in capitals.

<u>COMPUTER UNIT ACCESSORIES</u>

Decollators	VDU Trolley	Fire Extinguisher
Bursters	Split Level Table	Security Entry System
Printout Paper Catch Basket	Printer Table	Screen Filter
Data Caddy	Operator's Chairs	Disk Sleeves
Anti-Static Mats	Copy Holders	Screen Filter
Fire Security Cabinet	Acoustic Covers	VDU Cleaning Kit

Exercise 28 Indented letter

Type the following letter in indented style, either setting a tabular stop five or six spaces in from the left margin or using the first preset tab stop.

Type the date on the right-hand side taking care to begin typing so that the wraparound does not take part of the line onto the next one. This tab stop may be reached by pressing the tab key until appropriate space is reached prior to the right-hand margin.

Today's date

Wilmorton Brothers Ltd.,
Rochdale Road,
OLDHAM,
Lancs.
OL6 4BF

Dear Sirs,

We thank you for your enquiry of yesterday requesting information about our word processing systems.

We now have pleasure in enclosing our literature but feel that it would be more helpful to you if our representative could arrange to visit you and demonstrate our equipment to you and your staff.

If you could complete the enclosed card indicating the date and time when this would be convenient to you we will arrange for our representative to visit you. If in the meantime you have any further queries please do not hesitate to contact me.

Yours faithfully,

J. Morton
Sales Manager

5.2 Decimal Tabulation

Most word processors are capable of lining up columns of figures so that all the decimal points appear in line under each other, thus making it easy for the figures to be added up.

£	£
34.56	65.45
134.94	156.56
1345.50	1340.95
1515.00	1562.96

Some machines allow the operator to change the 'terminator', i.e. the point at which the figures need to be lined up, so that if a column of figures does not have any decimal points, but only commas, for the thousands in the figures, then the machine can be asked to line these up instead of the decimal points. Alternatively a £ sign or a $ sign may be used as the terminator.

The terminator is the reference point which the machine uses. In non-numeric tabulations, the operator, having set the tabulator to a certain position, presses the tabulator key and the cursor will jump to the tabulated position set and begin to type from left to right. When a numeric or decimal tabulator stop is set, instead of the machine typing from left to right, it will type from right to left, until the terminator is pressed, be this a decimal point or a comma, as in the example shown.

13,400	15,450
113,455	115,480
——	——
126,855	130,930
——	——

A £ sign or $ sign can also be used as a terminator, but it is only advisable to do so when the figures after the £ sign or $ sign have a uniform number of digits, otherwise this will look untidy and will not provide a format which can be quickly added up.

£300	£350
£600	£700
£4000	£47000
$40	$60
$80	$90
$800	$80000

When a decimal tab is used this is indicated to the operator by a sign appearing on the status line. This is sometimes a letter 'N' to show the machine is in numeric mode, or a decimal point that appears immediately above the tab setting; this is sometimes shown in inverse video.

Exercise 29 Decimal tabulation

Type the following exercise, and display effectively, setting a numeric or decimal tab stop where you feel it would be needed.

VISIT VACATION KINGDOM   Stay overnight

Enjoy yourself   Treat your family to what they deserve

The following prices will show you how reasonable such a weekend packed with thrills and fun can be.

Accommodation at one resort area
1 September to 16 December

	$
Sharing breakfast with TV Stars–one night	72.00
Two nights–sharing double room	185.00
Resort Rendezvous	325.00
Camp Site–one night	28.00
Camp Site–two nights	49.00
Breakfast–Adults	6.00
–Children	5.00
Visit the High Jinks Water Park	
Admission	3.00
Share lunch with the Seals at the	
Water Kingdom	3.50
Chance your Luck–Pearl diving	
A pearl every time–what size?	
Whatever the size of the pearl the	
price stays the same	7.50

5.3 Communication Styles, and the Use of Indentations

Most businesses have a need to use a variety of written communication styles.

The situations where note forms are used include the preparation of speeches, outline notes for a Chairman's briefing prior to the Annual General Meeting and draft reports which are sent to other delegates after a conference. Examples of such layouts which have a series of numbered points, include schematic notes, pyramid points, or sub-paragraphs.

The style used for such notes is to set down the relevant point in a brief but understandable form. These points are numbered and sub-divided under relevant headings. The layout used for this involves the use of a main heading, followed by a section heading which is further divided into a series of numbered or lettered points.

ITEM 1   CAR PARKING

ITEM 2   INTRODUCTION OF WORD PROCESSORS

     (i) Hardware/Software

    (ii) Furniture

   (iii) Training and Staffing

        (a) Supervisory Grades

        (b) Operator Grades

        (c) Trainee Operator Grades

    (iv) Ergonomics

     (v) Union Negotiations.

The example given shows how the second point has been expanded upon. An alternative layout is to use lettered points only, as in the example below.

A. COMMUNICATIONS

    (a) LAN

    (b) FACSIMILE

        (a) LAN stands for Local Area Network. This is where a number of computers are linked together within a small area such as a building, office block or a factory. Information or programs can be exchanged between computers within the system so that a document can be typed in at one computer and sent to another as internal mail or it can be sent for printing out at a remote printer.

(b) FACSIMILE transmission is the sending of exact copies of documents over external telephone lines from geographically remote locations. It works in a similar way to a telex machine except the document does not have to be keyed in.

5.4 Temporary Margins/Indents

If it is necessary to use an indentation, as in sub-paragraphs, then a temporary margin known as an indent can be set. When the cursor reaches the right-hand margin it will automatically wraparound to the indent instead of the left margin setting.

This indent can be set in a number of ways, depending upon the system used, some of which are listed here.

1 A command which sets the left margin temporarily five spaces in from the original margin, by using the first preset tab stop. This will remain until a carriage return is pressed, in which case the operator has to reset the indent after every paragraph ending.

2 An indent can be set by positioning the cursor five or six spaces in and pressing the format command followed by the indent key. This will be indicated on the format line and the indent will remain until it is cancelled by the operator. If it is necessary to type between the left margin and the indent the cursor must be taken back to that point by the operator.

3 The text can be typed first and then a command given which insets the left margin for that portion of text marked, to the first tab stop.

4 The ruler line can be positioned immediately above the beginning of the text to be inset and new margins set and then again at the completion of that section the ruler/format line can be brought down and the margins reverted to the original settings.

On some systems the facility is available to set one indent only, with this being indicated at the point set on the status line (it can be shown as an I). If a second indent is required on the same line, the first one is automatically cancelled when the second one is set. This is to ensure that the typing point always returns to the one temporary margin. However, if two or more indents are required and the operator does not wish to use the tabular stops, then there are facilities whereby the text always returns to the left margin, but special printer codes can be inserted in the margin at the point where indents are required, (a printer code may appear as a code followed by a number, this being the number of spaces the line will be indented).

If it is later decided to change the style of the layout then it is possible to delete the indentation, and return all the text to the left margin. This can be achieved by simply executing the command to erase some or all of the indents. To do this the cursor is positioned over the indents and the deletion key is pressed followed by an indication of the number of indents to be removed, i.e. one as in the case of an indented paragraph, or all if this applies to the whole document. On some systems it is necessary to use the reformat command for the portion of text marked (see Section 5.6).

Exercise 30 Use of temporary margins

Type the following list of procedures for display in your Word Processing Unit. Use a 1" margin on the left and the right and a temporary margin for the sub-paragraphs.

OFFICE ROUTINE

In order to help formalise procedures for the booting up of the System and the storing of documents during the day, plus the closing down of the System at night personnel are asked to note the following suggestions.

1 That only the supervisor or her deputy boots up the system each morning.

2 That all work received into the Unit for typing is recorded on the electronic indexing system, before it is allocated to operators.

3 That all operators store or save their work every 20 minutes, this is a precaution in case of a breakdown, when operators have been known to lose all that day's typing because of a system failure.

4 That all work is printed out at least four times per day and that each group of operators keeps to the time allocated to it. This is to alleviate any pressure on the spooling and buffer process which is incorporated into the printers.

5 That all work, unless specifically requested by the author, be returned via the internal mail. In the event of an urgent assignment, the clerk may be telephoned and asked to collect his/her own processed work.

6 That all operators complete and save their last document before 4.15 pm and that any back up copies are taken before 4.30 pm.

7 The system will be closed by the supervisor at 4.45 pm.

8 That all operators cover their machines and file any floppy disks in the appropriate place.

Exercise 31 Use of temporary margins/indentations

Type the following schematic notes using the most appropriate means
of indentation.

---

1   LOCAL AREA NETWORKS

   1.1   PERSONAL COMPUTERS
   1.2   DEDICATED WORD PROCESSORS
      1.1.1   The sales of personal computers have expanded rapidly over the last five years, and not all sales have been to private consumers. Many have been to industrial users. However, with the expansion in information processing systems within organisations it is no longer feasible or economical to use personal computers in isolation. It is becoming increasingly necessary for these to be linked into the main office system so that the manager using a personal computer can also access the main sales ledger if necessary to see the names of the largest customers, even though hemaybeworkingonhisownpersonal computer using a graphics design program. He may want to know who the previous customers were because this may influence his design thoughts. A LAN will make it possible for him to access this information.

      1.2.1   It is essential that dedicated word processors can also communicate with the main data bank of information within an organisation, so that a word processing secretary can access the stock control records or accounting system to obtain information which needs to be inserted into a letter to a customer. Provided the word processor has been designed with regard to an open systems standard and it has serial communications outside the proprietary word processing system then this can be connected to a LAN, and this makes communication with the data bank possible.

5.5 Format/Reformat

Another word meaning the same as format is layout.

Layout is important because the overall appearance of the document determines how much attention the reader will give to it. Considering a writer has as little as three seconds to capture the reader's interest when a decision to read or not to read is made, it is very important that the word processing operator lays out the material in a format which is easy to follow.

This is done by means of layout. The newspapers have been aware of this fact for years and that is why an advertiser using the classified section where hundreds of small advertisements appear, all separated only by black lines, will pay an extra amount to have a blank space inserted before and after the black line, so that his advertisement looks different from the rest and therefore catches the attention of the reader.

The word processing operator has the following tools at their disposal, to make the layout attractive:

1 variations in width of margins,
2 column layout.
3 size of type,
4 the amount of white space between the blocks of type,
5 bold type,
6 sub paragraphs and sub sections,
7 side by side typing,
8 special print functions,
9 change of style of type by changing the daisy wheel so that a written effect may appear.

5.6 Reformatting

The difference between reformatting and formatting is that reformatting is carried out after the document has been typed.

This is usually to achieve an effect whereby one paragraph or section is made to stand clear of all others in the text. Reformatting is carried out for various reasons:

(i) to add interest to the content;
(ii) to draw the reader's special attention to this section, for instance in a curriculum vitae when part of the applicant's previous experience is particularly relevant to the job being applied for;

(iii) to separate a particular section because it refers to a part of a report which is still in the process of being researched;

(iv) to give display to an otherwise long list of typescript;

(v) to list special events.

The means of reformatting a document vary according to the machine used. As a general guide, the text is inset from both the left and the right margins, and this is achieved by the operator first marking the block of text to be inset in some way and then indicating the new position either by placing the cursor or by marking the text at that point and then giving the reformat command.

On some systems it is necessary to reformat each paragraph after insertions have been made. This does not mean insetting text—it merely accommodates any insertions into it. The command to do this differs from the reformatting command, but it is mentioned here simply because it is often referred to in operator manuals as reformatting— whereas this function is really relaying or relocating text and it requires only that one command key is pressed to reshape the lines so that they agree with the margin settings.

Because the text is often brought in from the margins (although the same function can be used to extend the text out into the margins), the length of the document is consequently altered. The operator may have to carry out a further function following reformatting and this is repaging the document to accommodate the extra length. If the margins have been brought in then each typing line will be narrower and more lines are needed to accommodate this.

The above explanatory paragraph occupies six lines of type using a margin setting of 1″ either side. It is now repeated below after reformatting with a margin setting of 2″ either side and instead of occupying six lines it now takes ten lines.

Because the text is often brought in from the margins (although the same function can be used to extend the text out into the margins), the length of the document is consequently altered. The operator may have to carry out a further function following reformatting and this is repaging the document to accommodate the extra length. If the margins have been brought in then each typing line will be narrower and more lines are needed to accommodate this.

Exercise 32A Reformatting

Using 1″ margin either side type the following and print from screen. Do not erase the screen when complete, but see below for further instructions.

CARE OF MACHINES

Word processors and computers, like all machines, need maintenance from time to time. This maintenance usually includes a service whereby a qualified engineer checks the moving parts, such as the disk drives and the printer head, and removes any dust which may have accumulated inside the machine by means of a special vacuum cleaner. Whilst this care will prolong the physical life of the hardware, operators can assist by taking the trouble to:−

Cover the machine each evening to prevent dust entering.

Keep the keys clean by using cotton wool buds which can be bought impregnated with special cleaning solution.

Clean the screen daily, again using specially prepared impregnated cloths and then polishing with a lint free cloth.

Exercise 32B Reformatting

Reformat the last three paragraphs so that they all appear inset 1″ from both margins, giving a margin of 2″ either side for this section of text. Print from screen.

Exercise 33A Reformatting

Type the following and save on disk. Call the document 'Instruct'.

INSTRUCTIONS TO OPERATORS

This set of instructions is given to every new operator in the Word Processing Unit.

It is intended as a guide only and operators are invited to approach the supervisor at any time regarding queries concerning the receipt, processing or retrieval of work. They are especially requested to attend the instruction sessions which are held between the hours of 0900 and 1000 hours on the first Monday in every month.

Each session will deal with a different aspect of the machine's operation each time and although these are primarily intended for staff with less then three months' service in this Department any operator can attend in order to up-date or consolidate their knowledge of the word processing system.

It would be appreciated, however, if the operator could in the meantime follow the suggested code of practice adopted within the Unit.

The system is booted up in the Data Processing Department each morning, therefore individual operators, after switching on their own machines, need only key in their identity code.

All work should be filed away after the completion of each document but in the event of a long piece of text this should be filed at periodic intervals of ten minutes throughout the keying-in of the document.

All printed hard copies are channelled through the supervisor's office for delivery and collection by appropriate staff. In the event of a document being required urgently, the author must seek special permission for the processing of this through the supervisor who in turn will liaise with the operator concerned. On no account should the operators take it upon themselves to accept and deliver the work to the clerk personally.

The latter instruction is not an attempt to prevent personal contact by operators with the authors—indeed this is encouraged. It is merely a safeguard against work being wanted 'yesterday', which becomes endemic in all organisations if this is allowed to happen. Therefore for the benefit of all operators, it is important that scheduling and receipt of work is undertaken by the supervisor and a formalised procedure adopted.

Exercise 33B Reformatting

Recall the passage entitled 'Instruct'. Reformat the fourth and fifth paragraphs so that they appear inset 2″ from both margins. Reformat the seventh paragraph so that it appears inset 1″ from both margins.
  Update the disk and print from disk.

5.7 Moving Text

One of the great advantages of word processing, particularly for journalists or authors, is the ability to move text.

A paragraph which appeared as the first paragraph in a document can become the last paragraph, or one placed in the middle of the document can be placed at the end of the document.

Text can also be moved from side to side, i.e. horizontally, as well as vertically.

A portion of text can be moved up and across, down and across, or anywhere within the page.

How this is done will vary with each system, but generally the portion of text to be moved needs to be marked in some way, and the amount of this i.e. paragraph, block, or the beginning and end of the text, is marked. Sometimes it is possible to 'walk' the marked text with the cursor to the required position. On other systems it is necessary to mark the position to which the text is to be moved.

One thing to remember when moving paragraphs is to include the carriage returns at the ends of the text in the block marked to be moved. It is therefore advisable always to end a document with the statutory two carriage returns. This means that the operator does not have the problem of needing to insert an extra line space after repositioning the paragraph.

Exercise 34A Moving text

Using a 2″ margin either side type the following three paragraphs and save on disk. Call the document 'para'. Erase the screen and turn to the next page for further instructions.

This is the first paragraph to be typed in this piece of text. Later I may change my mind and make this the third paragraph.

This is the second paragraph and it appears in the middle of the three paragraphs at present.

This is the third paragraph and appears originally at the end of the document. The purpose of this exercise is to practise moving paragraphs, in a vertical direction.

Exercise 34B Moving text

Recall the document named 'para' and move the first paragraph so
that it becomes the third paragraph.
  Print from screen.
  Your work should appear as follows:

This is the second paragraph and it appears in the
middle of the three paragraphs at present.

This is the third paragraph and appears originally at
the end of the document. The purpose of this
exercise is to practise moving paragraphs, in a
vertical direction.

This is the first paragraph to be typed in this piece
of text. Later I may change my mind and make this
the third paragraph.

Do not erase the screen but see below for further instructions.

Exercise 34C Moving text

Still working on the document named 'para', you will see that the text
does not make sense now that the paragraphs have been moved.
  Move them back to the original position.

Exercise 35A Examination passage

Type one copy of the following letter using equal margins of 1″ (25 mm). Use today's date. When you have finished typing the task do *not* print out but save the document.

Miss Joan Linton,
Leisure Industries Ltd.,
Peterborough Road,
BRADFORD
BR2 4YZ

Dear Madam,

We thank you for your letter of yesterday concerning your executive Mr. James Jones, who is travelling to Miami.

Upon arrival Mr. Jones will be met by our representative and taken in our courtesy bus to the Tulip Inn for the first overnight stay. The following morning a representative from our associated company of car hirers will meet him at the hotel and deliver the car chosen. This car will be at Mr. Jones's disposal for the whole of his visit to the U.S.A., until his departure from Washington.

On the day of his departure Mr. Jones may deposit the car at our Algrave Service Station approximately two miles south of Washington International Airport; the courtesy bus will then transport him to the airport.

Further details are contained in the itinerary which is being sent to you together with the air tickets and foreign currency.

Yours faithfully,

Reproduced by kind permission of NWRAC Examinations Board. This formed part of the NWRAC/ULCI Word Processing Grade II Examination, June 1985.

Exercise 35B Examination passage

Recall the letter addressed to Miss Joan Linton and make the amendments shown. Update the document and print from disk.

Miss Joan Linton,

Leisure Industries Ltd.,

Peterborough Road,   *Insert the heading*

BRADFORD

BR2 4YZ   *Fly Drive*

Dear Madam,

We thank you for your letter of yesterday concerning your executive

Mr. James Jones, who is travelling to Miami, *Florida*.

Upon arrival Mr. Jones will be met by our representative and ~~taken~~/*transported* in our

courtesy bus to the Tulip Inn/*Miami Beach* for the first over-night stay. The following

morning a representative from our associated company of car hirers *Algrave Ltd* will ~~meet~~

~~him at the hotel and~~ deliver the car chosen.   This car will be at

Mr. Jones's disposal for the whole of his visit to the U.S.A., until his

departure from Washington.

On the day of his departure Mr. Jones may deposit the car at our

Algrave Service Station approximately two miles south of

Washington International Airport; the courtesy bus will then transport him to

the airport.

Further details are contained in the itinerary which is being sent to you

~~together with the air tickets and foreign currency.~~

Yours faithfully,   *We take this opportunity to remind you that our choice of cars is extensive and all vehicles are fully automatic.*

Reproduced by kind permission of NWRAC Examinations Board. This formed part of the NWRAC/ULCI Word Processing Grade II Examination, June 1985.

Exercise 36A

Type one copy of the following letter using equal margins of 1″ (25 mm). Use today's date. When you have finished typing the task do *not* print out but save the document.

Mr. James Leyland,
Advertising Services Department,
Richmond Manufacturing Co. Ltd.,
Steven Road,
LEYLAND
OL9 6PD

Dear Sir,

In reply to your letter regarding sponsorship, I now have pleasure in submitting a report which explains the advantages of sponsorship for the advertiser and the activity sponsored.

The popularity of sponsorship is growing and has been well documented while the history of it lies in the form of charity donations.

Its biggest advantage is the amount of air time an Organisation receives. A large computer company, with an advertising budget of £200,000, said that this would buy only a few thirty-second advertising spots on T.V. at £1,000 per second, but when they chose to sponsor a major sporting event and their name appeared around the track for the whole of the T.V. coverage, they managed to gain intervals totalling far more air time. The sporting event was also televised not only in the U.K. but also in 7 other western countries, therefore this computer company achieved some global advertising too.

Yours faithfully,

Exercise 36B

Recall the letter addressed to Mr. James Leyland and make the amendments shown. Update the document and print from disk.

Mr. James Leyland,

Advertising Services Department,

Richmond Manufacturing Co. Ltd.,

Steven Road,

LEYLAND

OL9 6PD

Insert the heading
SPONSORSHIP

Dear Sir,

In reply to your letter regarding sponsorship, I now have pleasure in submitting a report which explains the advantages of sponsorship *both* for the advertiser and the activity sponsored.

The popularity of sponsorship is growing and has been well documented *while* the history of it lies in the form of charity donations. *Of this is in the vast amount of literature on the subject.*

Its biggest advantage is the amount of air time an Organisation receives. A large computer company, with an advertising budget of £200,000, said that this would buy only a few thirty-second advertising spots on T.V. at £1,000 per second, but when they chose to sponsor a major sporting event and their name appeared around the track for the whole of the T.V. coverage, they managed to gain intervals totalling far more air time. The sporting event was ~~also~~ televised not only in the U.K. but also in 7 other western countries, therefore this computer company achieved some global advertising too.

Sponsorship is an arrangement between a business organisation and a particular sporting or leisure activity. The business organisation contributes money and in return receives advertising during the T.V. presentation of that event.

Yours faithfully,

5.8 Block and Column Movement

As well as moving paragraphs up and down the screen, columns or blocks of text can be moved from left to right. So if columns of figures, such as those presented below, need to be displayed in a different sequence, they can be moved.

The Sales figures for the last quarter show the following:

JAN	FEB	MARCH
30 000	40 000	60 000
30 000	60 000	10 000
20 000	80 000	20 000
80 000	180 000	90 000

The Accounts Department wish to see the figures in the order of the highest turnover rather than in chronological order as displayed above.

This can be achieved by selecting the column to be moved, placing a marker at the beginning of the column and also at the end, then placing a marker at the position to which the column is to be moved:

*JAN	FEB	MARCH
30 000	40 000	60 000
30 000	60 000	10 000
20 000	80 000	20 000
80 000	180 000	90 000
*		*

Alternatively, the margins are placed around the column to be moved, and it is now walked with the cursor to the required position. If this method is used then the operator must remember to move the margins back again to their original position after moving the block, otherwise editing will not be possible on text which appears outside the margins.

L R		
JAN	FEB	MARCH
30 000	40 000	60 000
30 000	60 000	10 000
20 000	80 000	20 000
80 000	180 000	90 000

This is how the columns would appear after the move:

FEB	MARCH	JAN
40 000	60 000	30 000
60 000	10 000	30 000
80 000	20 000	20 000
180 000	90 000	80 000

5.9 Double Column Layout

On a word processor it is relatively easy to achieve a newspaper style of layout, where blocks of text appear side by side.

Each block can also be justified to give a column effect, with each column having a straight right-hand edge.

It is possible using this type of layout to produce bilingual reports, or multilingual promotional material. Since each block of text can be moved independently of the other it is possible to place the native language of the country to which the promotion is addressed in the first column. Therefore if a company is sending advertising or promotional material to a West German customer, the text which would appear first on the paper, i.e. in the top left-hand column, would be the German text even though all the other languages would appear on the same sheet. If the next customer to be addressed resides in Italy, then it is an easy matter to move the Italian text to this position. This makes the customer feel that even though he is dealing with an organisation which sells its products internationally, it considers his country important enough to place the literature first on the paper.

This is also a layout which can be used in tourist literature, where two or three different languages are required on one leaflet.

It is extremely useful when typing balance sheets. Assets can be typed on one side of the paper and liabilities on the other; then if a different format is required for the Company Accounts, e.g. a vertical balance sheet, the assets can be easily positioned above the liabilities. This is sometimes used, when a company prefers a horizontal balance sheet for internal purposes, but adopts a more up to date layout for the published material such as Company Reports presented at the Annual General Meeting.

Double column layout is created by positioning both margins within the left-hand half of the paper. This becomes a relatively short typing line which does not extend beyond the middle of the page. A narrow margin of approximately ½″ is left clear down the centre of the page, and then the margins are reset in the right-hand half of the paper. This gives the appearance of two columns of text, both starting at the same level.

The two columns remain independent of each other and, before any editing can take place, the margins must be placed around the column to be edited, or moved.

The left-hand block is normally typed first and then both margins are moved to the right of the centre of the page. Often it is necessary to move the right-hand margin setting before the left, because the word processor may refuse to move the left margin beyond the setting of the right, and if the right-hand margin is positioned in the middle of the paper, then the left margin can not be moved beyond it.

The layout looks most attractive if even left- and right-hand margins are used and the centre space is approximately half the width of one of the margins. For example, if the left- and right-hand margins are 1″, then the centre margin should be approximately ½″. Since ½″ represents six spaces across if the machine is in twelve character pitch then three spaces should be positioned left of the centre and three spaces right of centre.

One consideration which should not be overlooked, is whether the text needs to be justified. Some machines place symbols on the screen to indicate this. These symbols may appear on the left of the text, so enough space should be allowed in the centre to accommodate them.

Exercise 37A Double column layout

Using A4 paper, type the following using the layout shown.

Make each block approximately the same width. If using a pitch of 12 spaces to the inch, leave a left and right-hand margin of 1″ and a centre margin of ½″. This means that each headed block should be approximately 35 characters across, therefore set the left margin at 12 and the right margin at 47.

Type the first block entitled Product leaving two carriage returns at the end of the block.

Now move the right-hand margin to 88 and the left-hand margin to 53. This page format should appear as follows:

L	R	L	R
12	47	53	88

Type the block entitled Place, leaving two carriage returns at the end of each line.

Move the left and right-hand margins back to 12 and 47 and type the block entitled Price, ending with two carriage returns.

Move the right-hand margin to 88 and the left to 53 and type the block entitled Promotion.

Save the document.

THE MARKETING MIX

The marketing mix is made up of the four 'P's, Product, Place, Price, Promotion.

PRODUCT

The product is one of the most important elements in marketing and selling because if the product is no good then it will not sell more than once in spite of all the marketing efforts. However, the marketing men can make quite a mundane product very attractive by giving it what is called the unique selling proposition. The unique selling proposition is some attribute which is added to it to make it stand out from all similar products, i.e. they suggest that the formulation is close to a natural pH balance.

PLACE

This really concerns where the product will be sold, but more specifically how it will be distributed. Will it be sold through wholesalers or through agents as some cosmetics are? Where is the right place to sell a product or service? It is not always the High Street. For instance in selling garden furniture it has been proved that out of town sites where the rates are lower and there is more space for car parking are a better proposition. There is now a great demand for empty spaces outside towns for selling.

PRICE

Not all products are sold on price alone. Indeed most are sold on their value. Whether this is real or imaginary it is the value of the product which is perceived by the customers which is sometimes enhanced by the marketeers. The price must give a profit which will cover the seller's production costs. If competitors are offering a similar product at a lower price, the seller will have to find a way to reduce his costs, in order to reduce his price and make his product competitive.

PROMOTION

All products need to be promoted one way or another. The most common ways of doing this are through direct advertising, in the press, on the radio, cinema or T.V. if the marketing budget is large enough. Sales promotion means issuing special offers or free samples or coupons with money off. A large company will usually conduct two or three sales promotions per year in order for them to keep pace with the rest of their competitors in that market, and keep their market share.

Exercise 37B Editing double column layouts

Edit the document called Marketing Mix, as shown.

Remember to place the margins around each block of text before editing that block.

THE MARKETING MIX

The marketing mix is made up of the four 'P's, Product, Place, Price, Promotion.

PRODUCT

PLACE

The product is one of the most important elements in marketing and selling because if the product is no good then it will not sell more than once in spite of all the marketing efforts. However, the marketing men can make quite an mundane product very attractive by giving it what is called *N.P.* the unique selling proposition. [The unique selling proposition is some attribute which is added to it to make *the rest of the products* it stand out from all ~~similar~~ *in that range* ~~products~~, i.e. they suggest that the *in selling shampoo* formulation is close to a natural pH balance/, *and therefore more beneficial because it has a 'natural' balance*

This really concerns where the product will be sold, but more specifically how it will be distributed. Will it be sold through wholesalers or through agents as some cosmetics are? Where is the right place to sell a product or service? It is not always the High Street. For instance in selling garden furniture it has been proved that out of town sites where the rates are lower and there is more space for car parking are a better proposition. There is now a great demand for ~~empty~~ *shopping sites* ~~spaces~~ outside towns ~~for selling~~.

PRICE

Not all products are sold on price alone. Indeed most are sold on their value. Whether this is real or imaginary it is the value of the product ~~which~~ *as it* is perceived by the customers, which ~~is sometimes enhanced by the marketeers~~. The price, must give a profit which will cover the seller's production costs. If competitors are offering a similar product at a lower price, the seller will have to find a way to reduce his costs, in order to reduce his price and make his product competitive.

→ the marketeers create and enhance, in other words the image.

PROMOTION

All products need to be promoted one way or another. The most common ways of doing this are through direct advertising, in the press, on the radio, cinema or T.V. *in full please* if the marketing budget is large enough. Sales promotion ~~means~~ *includes* issuing special offers ~~or~~ *i.e.* free samples *being given* or coupons with money off. A large company will N.P. usually conduct two or three sales promotions ~~per~~ *a* year in order for them to keep pace with the rest of their competitors in that market, *in this way they* and keep their market share.

Update the document and print out.

Practise moving the blocks.

Remember to position the margins around the blocks to be moved or, if your system requires it, use markers to indicate the block to be moved and markers to show where the block is to be moved to, so that the blocks of type appear in the following sequences:

PLACE   PRODUCT

PROMOTION   PRICE

Print from screen.

Now place the blocks in the following order:

PROMOTION   PRICE

PLACE   PRODUCT

Print from screen.

Recall the original document and re-position the blocks of type as follows:

PROMOTION   PRODUCT

PRICE   PLACE

Print from screen.

Test Yourself

The following questions relate to the functions explained in the last section. Try to answer them without consulting your notes. They concentrate upon the practical applications of the machine, so it is suggested that you write down the function keys you would press on your own machine in order to carry out the following tasks. Remember to check your answers with your own personal manual or alternatively perform the functions on the machine, using your answers.

1 How do you:
    (a)   move a paragraph from the bottom of the page to the top;
    (b)   move a column of figures across the screen;
    (c)   reformat a document to bring the text in six spaces from both the left and the right-hand margins;
    (d)   set an indent;
    (e)   cancel an indent;
    (f)   set a tab;
    (g)   clear a tab;
    (h)   set a decimal tab;
    (i)   change a decimal tab, so that the commas line up instead of decimal points;
    (j)   type in a newspaper style with blocks side by side?
2 What do you understand by 'reformatting'?
3 Give two examples when double column layout may be used.
4 Give an example when a temporary margin may be used.
5 Explain what is meant by decimal tab stops.
6 What does a LAN do?
7 What is meant by 'format'?
8 Why is it advisable for operators to save their work at frequent intervals throughout the day?
9 Give two examples when the 'move facility' is particularly useful in word processing.

PART V

DISK MANAGEMENT II

Chapter 6

Permanent Store Documents

6.1 Assembling

Assembling is the joining together of a set of commonly used phrases and the building of these into a letter.

We do this everyday, both in writing and in speaking, by using the same group of words. An example of some of the phrases which we all use may be in the opening paragraph of a letter, which we often begin:

'We thank you for your letter of'

or the closing paragraph, which gives the recipient the opportunity to ask for further details:

'If you would like any further information, please do not hesitate to contact us'.

It is possible to type these phrases once and then save each separate phrase as a document. When the operator needs to use one of these phrases the cursor is positioned, or a marker is placed, where the phrase is required. The disk is addressed by pressing the appropriate key and the phrase is brought from the disk on to the screen. The operator should notice here, that the function to assemble is different from recalling a document on to the screen. If a document is recalled to the screen it will automatically overwrite anything which is on the screen at that time, whereas assembling merely adds the named document to the text already showing on the screen.

Exercise 38A Saving standard phrases

Type the following phrases and save each one on disk as a separate document. Do not include the numbers of the phrases—these are used here merely to separate one phrase from another. When completed turn to Exercise 38B for further instructions.

1   We thank you for your letter

2   We now have pleasure in enclosing our catalogue

3   If you have any further queries do not hesitate to contact us

4   If you would like a demonstration of this product, we should be pleased to arrange this at your convenience.

5   Yours faithfully,
    ATHERTON PRODUCTS LTD.

P. R. McLain
Sales Manager

Exercise 38B   Assembling standard phrases

Type the following letter. When the phrase or sentence appears in brackets, do not type this but assemble it from disk. When the exercise is completed, print from screen.

Dear Sirs,

(We thank you for your letter) of the 5th July enquiring about our products. (We now have pleasure in enclosing our catalogue) and price list but should like to point out that we specialise in custom-built products and that delivery on these can be as early as four weeks from receipt of a firm order. (If you have any further queries please do not hesitate to contact us.) I shall be away from the office, however, for two weeks in August for my annual summer leave but you may leave a message with my secretary. My deputy will contact you and I will take up the matter on my return.

(If you would like a demonstration of this product we should be pleased to arrange this at your convenience.)

(Yours faithfully,
ATHERTON PRODUCTS LTD.

P. R. McLain
Sales Manager.)

6.2 Library Documents

A library document in word processing terms is a collection of documents or part documents (sometimes consisting of only two or three lines of type or even two or three words) which are stored on disk for future use in assembling complete texts.

These include words which are frequently used in the organisation but which are difficult to spell, e.g. medical terminology, or terminology specifically used in engineering, physics or chemical formulae. Whilst some word processing programs incorporate a spelling or dictionary function, those which do not can use the library document facility to achieve the same objective. The spelling and dictionary functions are explained in Section 6.4.

Library documents can also be used to store letter headings of the organisation, for instance the county council or the local authority may have different printed note paper for each department.

Whilst all printed stationery will include the county's or town's coat of arms, the Sports and Recreation Department may have a different address from the Department of Health and Welfare, and different named officials shown on the letter head, even though they both come under the auspices of the same authority. Instead of the authority using pre-printed stationery in such instances, they use high quality plain paper and the word processing operator calls up the library document which stores the appropriate letter head for the department in question. All the addresses are prepared on disk and these are called to the screen to form part of the letter. Any special print functions used, such as bold type or proportional spacing, means that the letter heading can have a professional finish even though it is not professionally printed. Some of the biggest advantages offered by such a system are:

(i) it eliminates the need to store several letter headings within one organisation, but provides the means for each department to use its own stationery, which can give the names of the executives specific to that department together with their telephone numbers and extension numbers;

(ii) if the executives within the department change frequently then these can be quickly updated on disk, without rendering large stocks of letter headed stationery obsolete;

(iii) the printer can be loaded with the same paper for every department and each operator can access each department's letter headings on the disk and select the appropriate one without the need to physically change the paper in the printer.

Library documents can also be used for signature clauses. In many cases these do not merely consist of two words such as Yours faithfully, but rather three or four lines, e.g:

Yours faithfully,
THOMPSON, PATEL AND MISTRY,

H. Mistry, B.A. (Hons). Dip. Inst. M.
Publicity Officer.

This simple close consists of 100 keystrokes or 100 characters. By having this already prepared on disk ready to bring into a document a considerable reduction of effort is achieved. Moreover, it is stored correctly on disk and there is no chance of inaccuracies appearing within it, which would not be the case if the operator had to key it in each time.

Standard paragraphs are also stored as library documents, these may consist of the opening and closing paragraphs used in quotations, e.g:

'We thank you for your enquiry and now have pleasure in enclosing our quotation.'

'If you have any further queries please do not hesitate to contact us.'

'We look forward to receiving your order.'

These paragraphs are stored on disk and given a name or a number.

As well as saving time and work for the word processing operator, this can also save author's time, because they simply dictate or write the number of the paragraph in their manuscript, instead of continually repeating the much used phrases.

6.3 Organisation and Storage of Library Documents

If the organisation is small and operators are using stand-alone machines, then the paragraphs stored as library documents may be left to the discretion of the individual operators and may consist only of the day's date, stored each day to eliminate the need to type it on each letter. However, if the organisation is large then the naming and cataloguing of standard paragraphs becomes a matter for the supervisor, because a formalised procedure becomes necessary if all operators are accessing the same central store of documents on disk.

Disk space is often at a premium and the library documents should be continually updated and all operators informed of such updates. Strict control should be maintained over any deletions or insertions made in such documents.

To illustrate the importance of this, one organisation which had several business partners found, after the sudden death of one of the key executives, that the word processing operator prepared a letter with the signature clause bearing the deceased's name. This happened simply because the disk had not been updated and the operator, assuming the library document to be correct, inserted this into the text.

Practical aspects of preparing and storing library documents

Apart from the organisation of which documents are stored on disk, and their indexing and continual updating, the question arises of the size of margins to use when preparing them.

Since each standard paragraph may be assembled into documents which have various margin settings, the library document should be typed with a margin setting of one on the left and the typing line should not extend beyond 70 or 76. This means that on an A4 sheet, which will accommodate 100 characters from edge to edge of the paper using elite pitch, there is a tolerance of 24 spaces. This will take care of the relatively standard 1″ margins either side. If on the other hand a procedure of standardised margins for every document is used within the organisation then the library document should be stored on the same margins as these.

Depending upon the system, the library document is typed and each phrase is stored as a separate file, being given a unique name or number. Then when the operator wants to access it and assemble it into a document, the cursor is positioned at the appropriate place and the command to assemble is given, followed by the name of the file. The execute key is pressed and the clause or sentence is added to the text on the screen. Note that the contents of the screen are not over-written as they would be with the recall function, they are merely added to.

It should be mentioned here that library documents are used as the letter is typed, i.e. as the text proceeds, and the stored phrase or sentence is inserted into the document as the operator approaches the need for it. If, however, there is a need to insert such a library document into the text after it has been typed, then on some systems space will need to be made for it. On other systems, the insert mode may take care of this and allow the operator to insert the library document in the middle of a piece of text. Once brought on to the screen, however, the library document may need to be reformatted, i.e. the margins changed to line it up with the margins of the text on the screen (see Section 5.6).

Another method of storing library documents, however, is to store several on one file. Each document is given an identifier which is sometimes a coded instruction followed by the first two letters of the word or phrase of the library document. A glossary is then set up which means that the machine will access that part of the disk every time the glossary key is pressed and the identifier code is typed. Therefore, whenever that word or phrase is needed the operator merely types the first two letters and presses a function key and the word is brought to the screen.

It is at this point that the new operator may become confused, because two or three different methods of achieving the same objective can be used and these will vary with each system. In an attempt to lessen any confusion, I should explain that the purpose of library documents is simply to store something on disk for later insertion into a piece of text and the terminology used to describe this function includes such terms as assembling, boiler-plating, cut and paste and the glossary function.

Either each document can be stored as a separate file, or each one may have a separate code, but reside in the same file.

The easiest term used to describe the whole operation is that of cut and paste, and this may be viewed literally as someone preparing a collage consisting of a house with a car in the drive, and a tree shading it. The house, car and tree are all collected from different magazines and cut out, then they are pasted upon a piece of paper to obtain a complete picture.

Although simplistic in nature this example is an attempt to illustrate a very useful word processing function which can seem unduly complicated because of the range of terminology attached to it.

A Letter Heading as a library document

■ LE

LEISURE AND RECREATIONAL SERVICES DEPARTMENT
REDWAY COUNTY COUNCIL
CIVIC CENTRE
REDWAY
SHROPSHIRE

Mr. J. Whitehead, MInst.M   Mr. T. Blackthorn, Dip.Inst.M

Head of Leisure Services Division   Activities Advisor

How difficult-to-spell words may be used as library documents

■ ha haemoglobin■ bi bilirubin ■ pn pneumonia ■ ps psychology

How clauses e.g. in legal documentation may be used as a library document

■ AS   AS WITNESS the hands of the parties,

Signed   by   the   said   JOHN MACINTOSH in the presence of:—

....

of ....

....

Occupation ....

■ Represents the coded instruction. The above demonstrates what the screen version may look like when a library document is created. The codes and initial letters would not of course appear on the final document. The code instructs the machine to access the document named.

6.4 Glossary and Dictionary Functions

A glossary may consist of a collection of difficult-to-spell words or technical phrases which are often used within a particular organisation, e.g. medical terminology in a hospital.

The operator compiles the glossary by first typing in a code followed by separate identifiers for each word or phrase. The identifiers may consist of the first two letters of the word, and may appear as follows:

ac accommodation   bu business

These are saved on disk and then a further command is given to put this document into the background memory of the machine, i.e. a glossary is set up which tells the machine the name of the document where these words can be found. Each time the operator needs to use one of these words the identifier is typed and then a function key is pressed and the machine will complete the word. The advantage of this of course is that the operator does not have to continually look up the spelling.

The dictionary function works in much the same way. However, these self-compiled dictionaries should not be confused with the facility which is now available on some word processors whereby a dictionary is present in the software and after the operator has typed a piece of text a spelling check can be carried out. Here the machine checks the spellings by matching them against those in its memory, and any words which do not match are highlighted on the screen, thus drawing the operator's attention to the fact.

The machine will, however, highlight all proper names because these will not be present in the normal dictionary. Here the operator simply removes the highlighting.

6.5 Graphics—Line Drawing

When a word processing operator is asked to use graphics on the machine, this can generally be taken to mean the use of line drawing.

It is possible on most machines to use the cursor key and the code key to draw horizontal and vertical lines on the screen. On some systems this may entail the use of the underline key and the repeat key to obtain horizontal lines. However, most sophisticated word processing programs will allow the operator to draw lines vertically too. Usually the horizontal line appears on the screen as a continuous line, while the vertical line appears as a series of broken dots on the screen but gives a continuous line when printed out.

This function is used for the compilation of forms, which require ruled boxes, or for tables of figures which are ruled for clarity, or for display purposes, for instance to denote a space of a particular size, e.g. when leaving spaces for photographs as an estate agent's secretary may do when typing out specifications of houses for sale.

Exercise 39 Use of graphics/line drawing

Type the following specification of a house for sale. Leave a space of
1″ square for a picture of the house and also for the view taken from
the lounge window. Rule these squares using the graphics facility.

Detached Chalet Style House

1′   1″
┌──────────────┐   ┌──────────────┐
│   │   │   │
│   │   1″   ½″   │   │   1″
│   │   space   │   │
│   │   here   │   │
└──────────────┘   └──────────────┘

27 LINKS VIEW - ST. ANDREWS

4   Bedrooms
Gas Central Heating
Double Glazing
Cavity Wall Insulation
Impressive Views to Rear

This property is a well maintained
spacious family detached
house situated on the perimeter
of a small quiet development

Internal viewing strongly recommended.

6.6 Forms and Masks

In the section on printing mention was made of special commands to direct a document to a particular printer, e.g. if a memo needed to be typed then the document was directed to the printer which held the memo paper.

An alternative means of achieving the same objective is to use a 'mask' which is first prepared on the screen with block codes and markers where insertions need to be made. This is then saved on disk, and every time a memo form needs to be typed the mask for a memo is called upon the screen.

A mask is another name for a layout of a form and may appear as below.

The mask allows the operator to position the various items and the block code is reached simply by pressing the tabulator key. It also removes the necessity for the standard items to be continually retyped, i.e. To–From etc., as well as serving the purpose of a reminder to complete the items.

A mask is particularly useful for preparing invoices or orders. The operator must remember to save the completed document under its own name and not simply update the mask. This may involve duplicating or copying the document before amendment, on some systems. If the operator does not remember to do either of these two, when a memo next needs to be typed, and the mask is recalled, the completed memo will appear rather than a blank memo form.

The same principle can be applied when a chart or rows of figures need to be bordered by a framework of horizontal or vertical lines:

PRODUCT	VOLUME	VALUE
Disk Boxes	10 000	20 000
Diskettes 5¼"	5 000	15 000
Cleaning Solution	4 000	2 000
Print Wheels	1 000	5 000
Multi-Strike Ribbon	6 000	30 000

If this table is reproduced at the end of each trading period then the blank chart can be prepared using the graphics facility, and then saved on disk. However, this time instead of typing the figures within the mask, the contents can be typed first and then the mask can be overlaid around the figures.This function is used in conjunction with the assembling or boiler-plating function.

The stages in the preparation of such a mask are as follows.

1   After assessing the amount of space needed for each item, as with the chart above, the supervisor should work through the product list and allow as many spaces in the product column as the product name containing the largest number of letters.Then allowing for spaces between the columns, prepare the overlay and save this on disk.

2   After the figures have been typed the cursor can be positioned over the first column and the assembling function executed. In this way the overlay will not erase the work on the screen, but merely border it.

3   The completed chart can then be saved under a unique name and the original overlay kept on disk for use in the future.

Exercise 40A

Type the following document in double line spacing and save on disk.
 Call the document 'Disks'

NOTICE TO OPERATORS

Operators are respectfully reminded that it is their sole responsibility to care for the floppy disks which they use. This entails:—

Replacing them in the envelope after use and subsequently replacing them in the appropriate disk box. The disk boxes are kept in the locked cupboard which is on the right hand wall beside the window.

It is important that disks are returned to the correct box, and any master copies of standardised formats are returned to the disk box marked standard.

On no account must the protect shield be removed from these disks—if an occasion arises whereby the operator needs to duplicate one of the standard forms on this disk then a formal request should be made through the supervisor. On no account must a copy be taken without permission. To do so is an offence and in any event this will be brought to the notice of the supervisor and will result in an official warning. Since all operators have signed the official secrets act duplication of the forms could result in a breach of this also.

Exercise 40B

Recall the document named 'Disks', carry out the corrections shown.
Change to single line spacing and update the disk. Print from disk.

NOTICE TO OPERATORS — *centre heading & embolden*

the disks

Operators are ~~respectfully~~ reminded that it is their sole responsibility to
care for the floppy disks which they use. This entails:-

Replacing ~~them~~ *the disks* in the envelope after use and subsequently replacing them in
the appropriate disk box. The disk boxes are kept in the locked cupboard
which is on the right hand wall beside the window.

very
It is important that disks are returned to the correct box, and any master
copies of standardised formats are returned to the disk box marked
standard.

run on
On no account must the protect shield be removed from these disks - if an
occasion arises whereby the operator needs to duplicate one of the standard
forms on this disk then a formal request should be made through the
supervisor. On no account must a copy be taken without */authorised/* permission. To do so
is an offence and in ~~any~~ event *the of this being* brought to the notice of the
supervisor ~~and will result in~~ *will be issued* an official warning. Since all operators have
l.c. signed the official secrets act, duplication of the forms could result in a
breach of this also.

Exercise 41 Special print functions

Using A4 paper type the following menu—menu refers to the choice of meals available in this instance, not the menu used in word processing.

Display it so that it looks attractive, using any special print functions or layouts you think necessary.

Save on disk and print from disk.

SUNDAY   LUNCH

Homemade Vegetable Soup
Prawn and Egg Andalouse
Barbequed Mushrooms

Roast Sirloin of Beef & Yorkshire Pudding
Roast Leg of Lamb with Mint Sauce
Smoked Salmon and Prawn Salad
Cold Boiled Ham with Sweet Pickle

Roast Potatoes and Fresh Vegetables

Sherry Trifle
Fresh Cream Gateau
Apple Pie
Cheeseboard

Coffee

Exercise 42A Double column layout

Type the following balance sheet, using double column layout, to give a horizontal presentation of a balance sheet, and save the document under the name 'Balance'. Use double underscoring under the final totals.

J. W. RIBBLESWHITE & CO. LTD.

BALANCE SHEET AS AT 31st March 1988

LIABILITIES		£	ASSETS	£	£
Capital		10,000	FIXED ASSETS		
Add Nett Profit		2,000	Plant and Machinery	2,100	
			Motor Vehicles	4,000	6,100
		12,000	CURRENT ASSETS		
Less Drawings		1,500			
			Closing Stock	1,000	
		10,500	Debtors	400	
CURRENT LIABILITIES			Bank	200	
			Cash	300	1,900
Bank Overdraft	500				
Trade Creditors	2,000	2,500			
		£8,000			£8,000

Exercise 42B Double column layout and movement of columns

Recall the document called 'Balance' and move the assets so that they appear below the liabilities to give a balance sheet with a vertical presentation.

J. W. RIBBLESWHITE & CO. LTD.

BALANCE SHEET AS AT 31st March 1988

LIABILITIES

		£
Capital		10,000
Add Nett Profit		2,000
		————
		12,000
Less Drawings		1,500
		————
		10,500
CURRENT LIABILITIES		
Bank Overdraft	500	
Trade Creditors	2,000	2,500
		————
		£8,000
		═══════

ASSETS

	£	£
FIXED ASSETS		
Plant and Machinery	2,100	
Motor Vehicles	4,000	6,100
CURRENT ASSETS		
Closing Stock	1,000	
Debtors	400	
Bank	200	
Cash	300	1,900
		————
		£8,000
		═══════

Exercise 43 Proportional spacing

Using proportional spacing type the following extract from the Chairman's report.
  Save on disk and print from disk.

EXTRACT FROM THE CHAIRMAN'S REPORT

given at the A.G.M. held at the Head Office of the Company on

It is with great pleasure that I report upon the successful implementation of new technology both within the factory and also in the offices. This has been a time for enormous capital expenditure but I have no doubt that the returns which we will gain in reduced costs will justify every pound spent. What is more our staff are to be complimented upon their successful adaptation to their new working environment and the technology within it. We were fortunate in having a staff who, although of diverse ages, all shared a youthful enthusiasm for the change and willingness to co-operate with the management both in training and also in the transition from more traditional methods of office work to new and innovative techniques. We congratulate them all and express our appreciation for their goodwill during a very difficult transitionary period.

Exercise 44A Change of character spacing—printer codes

Using a character pitch of 10 to the inch, i.e. pica type, type the following three paragraphs in single line spacing. Insert special printer codes to change the character pitch to 13 characters to the inch for the second paragraph only.

Save the document on disk, call it 'Video' and print out a hard copy.

This conference is the 33rd to be held by this Association and it is with great pleasure that we welcome once again Miss Fiona McBride, M.A.

Fiona McBride is to speak upon the developments in electronic communication and take us into the future with a spectacular graphical demonstration of the features in the new office complex in Dallas, Texas, U.S.A.

A copy of the video used by Fiona McBride together with a recording of her lecture will be available to conference delegates only.

Exercise 44B Change of line spacing

Recall the document called 'Video' and insert a printer code to change the second paragraph to 1½ line spacing.

Update the document and print out a hard copy.

Test Yourself

1 What do you understand by a library document?
2 What does the graphics facility do on a word processor?
3 Give two examples when the graphics facility may be useful.
4 Explain what is meant by a dictionary function.
5 Explain how a word processing operator may use the dictionary function.

PART VI

ADDITIONAL WORD PROCESSING FUNCTIONS

Chapter 7

Listing and Merging, Search and Replace, Pagination

7.1 Standard Letters and Standard Forms

As all office workers will no doubt be aware, standard letters and standard forms have been used in offices of all organisations for many years. The advent of the word processor simply made it easier for these standard forms and letters to be created and also made it especially easy to complete them. Whereas standard forms and letters used to be typed and reproduced in vast numbers with spaces left for details or variables to be later inserted on to each individual sheet, word processors eliminate the need to store hard copies and have also made it possible to store, on disk, lists of details or variables that the word processor will insert automatically, thereby giving the appearance of a letter which has been prepared solely for the addressee.

An organisation can now have a list of all the names and addresses of its customers, clients, suppliers and shareholders ready on disk which can then be merged with a standard letter.

Before standard letters can be merged with a given set of variables, it is necessary that a 'list' of variables is prepared. This is prepared by the operator keying in the names and addresses of all correspondents, and saving these on disk. A block code or angle bracket, depending upon the system, is used to separate one set of variables from another, that is the name and address may constitute one set of variables and these are separated from perhaps the date or time of an appointment. These items, as the name 'variables' implies, will vary with each letter typed.

The standard letter is then typed in and the corresponding block codes or angle brackets are placed where the variables need to be inserted. This document is also saved on disk under a different name.

For the purposes of this example we will assume that the name of the document containing the variables is 'Customer' and that the name of the standard letter is 'Product'. On most systems, the merging of these two documents is achieved by giving the appropriate command (check with your operator's manual) to merge the document named 'Customer' with the document named 'Product'; the merging takes place automatically i.e. the variables are inserted into the appropriate places which are marked in the letter by the block codes or angle brackets.

The completed letters can be printed out immediately they are merged, using continuous stationery so that the first letter is merged with the first set of variables and printed out and whilst this is taking place the machine is automatically merging the next letter with the second set of variables.

Alternatively, on some systems the merging can take place in the background memory and the completed letters are saved on disk in a separate file, ready for printing at a later stage. The standard letter document and the variables document remain on disk unaltered and both can be used again, or the same set of variables can be used with a new standard letter.

On some systems it is possible to use the same set of variable information for the envelope or address label. However, some adjustment may be needed to the list so that the machine will override the instruction to insert all the variables and merely select the ones needed. For instance, the date and time of an appointment may be present as part of the variables but these would obviously not be required on the envelope.

The list of variables often constitutes the organisation's mailing list, which could be invaluable in the hands of a competitor. Although many market research companies provide mailing lists of potential customers or target markets, these cost money, and even the organisation's own mailing list has probably been built up over many years; therefore it represents a valuable investment in time alone. With this in mind, it must be treated as a confidential document and the disk should be categorised as one which must not be copied without the permission of the supervisor.

As word processing systems become more sophisticated and are integrated into the whole filing system of the organisation, the word processing operator will gain access to the organisation's data base which, for the purposes of this example, will hold a collection of all the names and addresses of the customers with which the organisation trades.

This information store is used as a basis for selection of all the variable data which is needed to address a customer. Whilst the sales department may be using this same data base to examine the sales areas with the highest profit figure, the word processing operator can be using the same set of records to extract the names and addresses of all customers located in a particular geographical area. Once having extracted these, by using a selection procedure whereby the machine is asked to extract all addresses which end in Greater Manchester, the operator can use these to create the 'list' in preparing the variables page which can later be merged into a standard letter.

Let us assume for the purposes of this example that the standard letter is to invite all customers in the Greater Manchester area to a luncheon party, where a new product of the company will be launched. The variables page is already partially prepared, in that all the names and addresses are extracted from the data base, and can be added to the other variables needed to inform the customer of the date and time of the luncheon. These are saved as a separate document, and constitute the 'list'. All that is now required is for the word processing operator to type and save the standard letter on disk, then by using the listing and merging facility a large number of letters, which all appear to have been typed as separate invitations, can be mailed to all customers in the Greater Manchester area.

Letter of invitation to a product launch

Standard letter called 'Product'

☒

☒

Dear ☒

It is with great pleasure that we invite you to attend a luncheon party to be held in the Adams Room at the Captain's Galley Hotel, Oak Avenue, Withington on ☒.

The luncheon is to mark the occasion of the launch of our latest innovation in automative production systems, namely the robotised goods mover, code named 'Robby'.

The guest speaker will be Mr John Williams, Chairman and Managing Director of Distribution Services Ltd, the company which worked closely with our design team and without whose help 'Robby' would not have been developed.

Our investment in this unique product has been considerable, both in time and money. However, we feel sure that you will agree with us when you see the uses to which 'Robby' can be put that this is a product you cannot afford to overlook.

Both our sales staff, with whom many of you are already familiar, and our designers, will be on hand to demonstrate the product. Should you decide to place an order a discount of 2% will be allowed on all orders received within 14 days of the product launch.

We look forward to meeting you at the luncheon.

Yours sincerely

Sales Manager

Variables for insertion into standard letter: document name 'Customer'

19 June☒
Mrs J D Rishworth
The Buyer
Fenton Supplies plc
Whitchurch Road
MANCHESTER☒Mrs Rishworth☒Thursday 20 July☒
19 June☒
Mr B C Brophy
Purchasing Officer
Fairway Products
Larne Street
BOLTON☒Mr Brophy☒Friday 21 July☒
20 June☒
Mr M McVale
Purchasing Officer
Nettle Supplies plc
ROCHDALE☒Mr McVale☒Wednesday 19 July☒

Example of completed letters after merging of the standard letter called
'Product' with the list of variables called 'Customer'

1   19 June

Mrs J D Rishworth
The Buyer
Fenton Supplies plc
Whitchurch Road
MANCHESTER

Dear Mrs Rishworth

It is with great pleasure that we invite you to attend a luncheon
party to be held in the Adams Room at the Captain's Galley Hotel,
Oak Avenue, Withington on Thursday 20 July.

The luncheon is to mark the occasion of the launch of our latest
innovation in automative production systems, namely the
robotised goods mover, code named 'Robby'.

The guest speaker will be Mr John Williams, Chairman and
Managing Director of Distribution Services Ltd, the company
which worked closely with our design team and without whose
help 'Robby' would not have been developed.

Our investment in this unique product has been considerable,
both in time and money. However, we feel sure that you will agree
with us when you see the uses to which 'Robby' can be put that this
is a product you cannot afford to overlook.

Both our sales staff, with whom many of you are already familiar,
and our designers, will be on hand to demonstrate the product.
Should you decide to place an order a discount of 2% will be
allowed on all orders received within 14 days of the product
launch.

We look forward to meeting you at the luncheon.

Yours sincerely

Sales Manager

2   19 June

Mr B C Brophy
Purchasing Officer
Fairway Products
Larne Street
BOLTON

Dear Mr Brophy

It is with great pleasure that we invite you to attend a luncheon party to be held in the Adams Room at the Captain's Galley Hotel, Oak Avenue, Withington on Friday 21 July.

The luncheon is to mark the occasion of the launch of our latest innovation in automative production systems, namely the robotised goods mover, code named 'Robby'.

The guest speaker will be Mr John Williams, Chairman and Managing Director of Distribution Services Ltd, the company which worked closely with our design team and without whose help 'Robby' would not have been developed.

Our investment in this unique product has been considerable, both in time and money. However, we feel sure that you will agree with us when you see the uses to which 'Robby' can be put that this is a product you cannot afford to overlook.

Both our sales staff, with whom many of you are already familiar, and our designers, will be on hand to demonstrate the product. Should you decide to place an order a discount of 2% will be allowed on all orders received within 14 days of the product launch.

We look forward to meeting you at the luncheon.

Yours sincerely

Sales Manager

3   20 June

Mr M McVale
Purchasing Officer
Nettle Supplies plc
ROCHDALE

Dear Mr McVale

It is with great pleasure that we invite you to attend a luncheon party to be held in the Adams Room at the Captain's Galley Hotel, Oak Avenue, Withington on Wednesday 19 July.

The luncheon is to mark the occasion of the launch of our latest innovation in automative production systems, namely the robotised goods mover, code named 'Robby'.

The guest speaker will be Mr John Williams, Chairman and Managing Director of Distribution Services Ltd, the company which worked closely with our design team and without whose help 'Robby' would not have been developed.

Our investment in this unique product has been considerable, both in time and money. However, we feel sure that you will agree with us when you see the uses to which 'Robby' can be put that this is a product you cannot afford to overlook.

Both our sales staff, with whom many of you are already familiar, and our designers, will be on hand to demonstrate the product. Should you decide to place an order a discount of 2% will be allowed on all orders received within 14 days of the product launch.

We look forward to meeting you at the luncheon.

Yours sincerely

Sales Manager

The list and selection of variables

In compiling the 'list' of variables, mention was made of the word processing operator using a data base from which this variable information was extracted.

A data base is a collection of facts and figures and can be compared to a filing system which is made up of sets of records or files which previously may have been stored in a card index box. Each card was a record and collectively the cards were a file. On each card certain key headings appeared e.g. a person's name and address, date of birth etc. In computing terms these key headings are known as 'key fields' or identifiers. Each card may have several identifiers.

The staff record card below shows items which can be used as identifiers, e.g. the person's name, job title, employment number, date of commencing employment with the company.

```
Employee's Name ........................................................
Address ...............................................................

        ...............................................................
D.O.B. ...........................................Tel. No. ..............
Job Title .......................................Employment No. ..........
Date of commencing work with this
Company ...............................................................
Title of Post held ....................................................
Department ............................................................
```

With computerised files, the records can be read and a selection procedure enacted which will extract all records which have a key field which matches the search criterion. For example a command can be given to search for and extract all records of an employee who has completed a length of service with the company greater than three years. The computer will search the date of commencement with the company and reject all those records which do not match the stipulated 'greater than three years' with the company. These can be used to form the 'list' which is merged with a standard letter inviting these personnel to attend the Head Office of the company for an appraisal interview.

An example is shown of the variables extracted and the standard letter inviting them for interview.

A standard letter inviting employees to attend the Head Office of the organisation for an interview

☒

☒

Dear ☒

As an organisation we are fortunate in having a large number of employees who are well educated and highly qualified and who have been with the Company for some time. As you are one of these persons we feel that it is very important that your talents are utilised to the full, both for your own personal benefit and satisfaction as well as for the growth and expansion of this Company.

It is with these facts in mind that we would like you to attend for a short interview on ☒ at ☒ so that the Management Team can review your performance and plan your future career to our mutual benefit.

We suggest that you inform your Section Leader of the date and time of the arranged interview and if this is inconvenient please do not hesitate to let us know, so that another appointment can be made for your appraisal interview.

Yours sincerely,

Personnel Officer

A set of variables extracted from the personnel file

15th August ☒
Mr. S. McFeeny,
26 Summervale,
Prehane Park,
LONDONDERRY,
Northern Ireland.☒Mr. McFeeny☒26th August☒1400 hrs.☒

16th August ☒
Miss D. M. Roberts,
35 Dundonald Avenue,
Colwyn Bay,
North Wales.☒Miss Roberts☒27th August☒1500 hrs.☒

16th August ☒
Miss J. Smith,
34 Winston Drive,
Worsley,
Greater Manchester.☒Miss Smith☒26th August☒1500 hrs.☒

Standard forms

The automatic listing and merging facility can be used in exactly the same way in the completion of standard forms as it was used for standard letters. However, it is also possible to complete both standard letters and standard forms manually.

The standard form or standard letter is typed. Block codes or angle brackets or other markers are placed where variables need to be inserted and then the document is saved on disk.

If the standard form or letter is completed manually by the operator, the block codes or other markers are reached by pressing either the tabulator key or a function key so that the cursor moves directly to the position where a variable needs to be typed in. Once having typed in the variable information, the operator repeats the operation and the cursor moves to the next block code or angle bracket.

When the form or letter has been completed with all the variable information, the document can be printed out directly from screen, or alternatively, saved on disk under a different name from the original standard form. This leaves the standard form or letter on disk unaltered so that it can be recalled for use on a future occasion.

Exercise 45A Preparation of standard form

Prepare the following form inserting block codes where the variables will be inserted. Save on disk.

HOTEL BOOKING FORM

Since all the bookings are computerised in this hotel, we should be pleased if you would complete and return the form below. We can assure you that this is for the comfort and convenience of our guests because only in this way can we ascertain your exact requirements. It is also a valuable management tool to assist our planning. As a business person yourself we are sure that you will understand the importance of this.

NAME

ADDRESS

NAME OF COUNTRY AND COMPANY

ROOM BOOKED	DOUBLE	SINGLE	TWIN
	SHOWER	BALCONY	BATH

DATE OF BOOKING	TO	FROM	
NEWSPAPER	NEW YORK TIMES	DAILY TELEGRAPH	
	LE MONDE	LE FIGARO	
CREDIT CARD	ACCESS	GOLD	VISA

Exercise 45B Form completion

Recall the hotel booking form and complete with the following details.

If merging these automatically, prepare the variables page first and save on disk.

If merging these manually then use the appropriate key to reach the block codes or angle brackets.

Print one hard copy.

Mr. J. Taylor

Hotel Imperiale, Via Venetto, Rome

Turin Italy—Fiat

Requirements: Single room with shower and balcony (indicate with a X)

To: 3.8.19--   From: 1.8.19--

Daily Telegraph

To pay by Access No. 5224 0600 6733 789

Exercise 46A Preparation of standard letter

Type the following letter, inserting the appropriate block codes/angle brackets where the variables will be inserted. Save on disk. Call the document 'Doctor'.

Dear

An appointment has been made for you to attend the Out Patients' Department at this hospital on   at

If you cannot keep this appointment we should be pleased if you would let us know as soon as possible so that another appointment can be made for you.

Yours faithfully,

Exercise 46B Preparation of variables for insertion into standard letter

Prepare variables for insertion into the standard letter in Exercise 46A. Prepare three letters all addressed to different patients. Use names and addresses of your own choice. The first patient is to attend the hospital on 1st January at 1030 hours. The second patient is to attend the hospital on 3rd January at 1300 hours, and the third patient is to attend the hospital on 4th January at 1330 hours.

Save the variables on disk. Call the document 'Patients'.

Exercise 46C Mail merge

Merge the variables prepared in Exercise 46B with the standard letter prepared in Exercise 46A and print hard copies addressed to each patient.

Exercise 47A Preparation of standard letter

Type the following letter, inserting the appropriate block codes/angle brackets where the variables will be inserted. Save on disk. Call the document 'Interview'.

Dear

OVERSEAS AGENT

We thank you for your letter of application for the above Post and should be pleased if you would attend for interview on
   at

Upon your arrival please report to Reception and ask for Miss Kelly.

If you are unable to attend we should be grateful if you would inform us as soon as possible so that alternative arrangements can be made.

Please bring with you a list of any other Principals you represent.

We look forward to meeting you in the near future.

Yours sincerely,

Exercise 47B Preparation of variables for insertion into standard letter

Prepare the variables given below and save on disk. Call the document 'Applicants'. They are all to attend for interview on 26th January. The first interviewee is to attend at 1300 hours and to be followed by the others at one hour intervals.

---

1   Brenda Williams
    10735-106 Street
    EDMONTON, Alberta
    Canada
    T6K 3B1

2   Au Frau
    Corinna Pless
    Wilschenbrucher Weg
    2130 Luneburg

3   Gent. Signora
    Antonella Campodall'Orto
    Via Ovidio 9
    34100 Padava

4   "Ingenieros Navales"
    Paseo de la Castellana, 129
    28114 MADRID

Exercise 47C Mail merge

Merge the variables prepared in Exercise 47B with the standard letter prepared in Exercise 47A and print hard copies addressed to each interviewee.

7.2 Search and Replace

There are many instances where this function is useful to the author and the word processing operator and even the simplest of word processing programs appears to incorporate this facility. However, as with many things there are variations on a theme and these include:

(i) a manual search function;
(ii) a manual search and replace function;

  (iii) an automatic search and replace function;

  (iv) a literal/automatic search and replace function;

   (v) a search function from the beginning of the document;

  (vi) a search function from the cursor to the end of the document;

 (vii) a search function from the cursor backwards to the beginning of the document;

(viii) a search function which requires searching for a given word and replacing this with either the same word or another word, which is emboldened or which needs to appear in uppercase.

As the name implies the machine is given an instruction to search for a word or phrase (in computer terms this is known as a search string) and once having found it, it usually indicates this to the operator by highlighting the word. It is then possible to give the machine an instruction to replace it with the typed-in replacement string. In operating this function for each search string, the operator has a choice, either to replace the word or to move on to the next occurrence of the word.

The search function only searches for the words and finds them, but does not replace them.

In using the automatic search and replace function, the machine is requested to find every occurrence of the word or phrase and replace this with another. This it will do either on the screen or in the background memory on the disk, but before using the automatic function the operator should be completely certain that every occurrence of the phrase needs to be changed.

A classic mistake can occur here, whereby the author decides to adopt a more democratic style and change all the I's to we's. It is possible that unless the machine is requested specifically to replace only the capital I's with a space on either side of them, it will change every letter 'i' in sight, and change words such as 'write' to 'wrwete' and 'time' to 'tweme'. In such an instance a literal search should be performed, whereby only those words which match exactly the search string are found and changed.

Items (v), (vi) and (vii) merely give the operator a choice of where to start and end the searching and replacing. In a report of twenty or more pages, this can be useful, because it may only be in the first five or six pages that the words occur, or perhaps in the recommendations at the end of the report, so there is no need for the machine to search through the whole document.

The function mentioned in item (viii) will differ according to the system used. On some word processing systems it is possible simply to set up a search string for the word or phrase and then set up a replacement string, together with the print commands to embolden it. This will not only replace the string but will also embolden it. However, on some systems the emboldening is not achieved so simply and it may mean that the search string is set up and then the operator must return to the menu and enlist the help of special utilities, that is create a 'user definition' which specifies that the word to be replaced is in a particular print, e.g. bold type.

The end result is the same—the means of achieving it will depend upon the word processing software. If such a facility is not available then the long way around this is to search for the string and replace it with the new string and then return to each occurrence of the replacement string and insert the printer commands to embolden the words or phrase. The operator's manual should be consulted here.

Some applications of the search and replace facility

It can be used as an aid in proof-reading. For instance the operator may want to check the spelling of a foreign name which appears in a long report. To ensure that it has been spelt correctly throughout the document, a search function can be set up to search for every occurrence of the word. This makes it unnecessary to scroll through the whole document merely to check the spelling of one word. In such an instance a manual search should be set up whereby the operator asks the machine to search for this word. Once this command is executed the cursor will move to the first occurrence of the word. Only if the word has been spelt the same way as the search string will the machine find it. Every time the machine finds this word the operator keeps count of these and then counts the number of times the word appears in the script. If the two do not match, then either the word has been omitted or alternatively it has been incorrectly spelt.

Another use of the search and replace function is that of updating product lists and catalogues. These often require minor changes, for instance, a product list containing the colours of household paints. The names and colours may be changed to accommodate changes in tastes and fashions. The colour 'off-white' may be replaced with 'misty white' and 'bright yellow' with 'sunshine gold'. These colours may appear on several lists, e.g. as gloss paint, emulsion paint with matt and silk finishes, etc. The use of search and replace to update them is much more efficient than the use of insert and deletion functions.

Search and replace can also be used to change the names of projects. In one case, in an architect's office a number of documents, including quotations and specifications, had been prepared for a client for the proposed project, which was the design and building of a new church to be named St. Steven's. After a short period of time the client informed the architect that the church was now to be named St. Paul's. This meant that all the documents already prepared had the incorrect project name. By using the search and replace function it was a simple matter to search the documents for St. Steven's and replace this with St. Paul's.

When staff lists need updating, again the search and replacement function can be invaluable. Members of a department may change frequently but the position and designation remain the same. An example is the position of Export Sales Manager. In one exporting company, the person holding this position was required to spend a period of time representing the company in other European countries. Therefore several persons held this position in the Head Office within a short period of time, and the staff list was continually revised.

After a draft copy of a report has been produced, the author may request the operator to insert a footnote at the bottom of every page where some abbreviation has been used, so that a lay person reading the report will not be confused. An example is the use of the abbreviation, 'F.E.' as a shortened version of 'Further Education'. The operator can search the document pages for F.E. and then insert a footnote explaining this at the bottom of each page where this occurs.

Exercise 48A   Examination passage

Type one copy of the following document using equal margins of 1″ (25 mm). Use today's date. When you have finished typing the task do *not* print out but save the document.

THEME PARKS

What are Theme Parks? To most of us the name conjures up images of a typical fun-fair atmosphere, traditional jingles, highly coloured carriages decked with squealing children and adults too; overhead cable cars, floating gracefully above the masses below; pink candy floss, the smell of hot dogs and newly baked pop corn.

Computer technology is now used extensively to control the nerve centre of many theme parks, and even the most humble of fun-fairs house few attractions which are not electronically operated.

The appearance therefore of the old Donkey Derby, where balls are rolled and the donkey moves a number of gallops along the track corresponding to the score of the hole the ball reached, strikes a nostalgic note for those old enough to remember these relics of a less sophisticated age.

Reproduced by kind permission of NWRAC Examinations Board. This passage is an adaptation of one which formed part of the NWRAC/ULCI Word Processing Grade II Examination, June 1986.

Exercise 48B Examination passage

Recall the document entitled 'Theme Parks' and make the amendments shown. Update the document. Print from disk.

Please change by search and replace —
Theme to Entertainment

THEME PARKS   *centre heading*
         Justify right margin

What are Theme Parks? To most ~~of us~~ the name conjures up images of a typical
persons
fun-fair ~~atmosphere~~, traditional jingles, highly coloured carriages decked
with
with squealing children and adults too; overhead cable cars, floating
         cheerful   *the sale of*
gracefully above the/masses below;/pink candy floss, the smell of hot dogs
and newly baked pop corn.

Computer technology is now used extensively to control the/nerve centre/of
many theme parks, and even the most humble of fun-fairs house few attractions
which are not electronically operated.

                    in Fantasy Fair   *or thrown*
The appearance therefore/ of the old Donkey Derby, where balls are rolled/and
the donkey moves a number of gallops along the track ~~corresponding to the~~
                                        people
~~score of the hole the ball reached~~, strikes a nostalgic note for those/old
enough to remember these relics of a less sophisticated age.

Fantasy Fair in Florida is a high class
fun-fair with entertainment of singing
and dancing, lazer and firework displays,
all set to music. It provides privileged
glimpses into the future, which are aided
by animations and computer graphics,
and all the latest electronic techniques.

Exercise 49A

Type the following exercise and save on disk.

PRODUCTS AND SALES

The Product Portfolio is a well-known business concept.

By product portfolio we mean the number of products which a company produces and product life cycle theory refers to the growth in sales as a new product matures and then declines so it needs to be replaced by new and more up-to-date lines.

Recently, however, there has been a new concept introduced into the marketing thinking, that of repeat cycle purchases. Whilst it may always have been true that the average household replaces a three piece lounge suite approximately every seven years, this does little to increase sales. However, with the increase in affluence and changing family life styles the marketeers have found that instead of households buying one T.V. set they now buy at least two, one for the adults and one for the children. Also the sets bought for children have been coupled with the purchase of personal computers, many of which have been sold without monitors, thereby necessitating a T.V. set as an additional item.

Another phenomenon has been the increase in the sales of fridges; this is not because people are stocking up more food but because more fridges are being bought by organisations other than households. For instance hotels and motels are installing fridges into all their bedrooms. So too are offices installing fridges for the use of their employees.

Exercise 49B

Recall the exercise entitled 'Products and Sales' and carry out the corrections shown.

Using the search and replace facility search for the word T.V. and replace this with television; search for the word fridge and replace this with refrigerator.

PRODUCTS AND SALES

The Product Portfolio *and the product life cycle theory* ~~is a~~ well-known business concept*,*s. *are*

By product portfolio we mean *and variety* the number *by* of products which a company produces and *product* life cycle theory *we mean* ~~refers to~~ the growth *rate* in sales *as* a new product *Products* matures and then declines so *it needs* to be *continually* replaced by new and more up-to-date lines.

Recently, however, there has been a new concept introduced into the marketing ~~thinking~~ *theory* that of repeat cycle purchases. Whilst it may always have been true that the average household replaces a three piece lounge suite approximately every seven years, this does little to increase sales. However, with the increase in affluence and changing family life styles the marketeers have found that instead of households buying one T.V. set they now buy at least two, one for the adults and one for the children. Also the sets bought for children have been coupled with the purchase of personal computers, many of which have been sold without monitors, thereby necessitating a T.V. set as an additional item.

Another phenomenon has been the increase in the sales of fridges; this is not because people are stocking up more food but because more fridges are being bought by organisations other than households. For instance hotels and motels are installing fridges into all their bedrooms *for the storage of drinks. This provides a mini bar for their guests.* So too are offices installing fridges for the use of their employees.

Exercise 50A

Type the following letter and save on disk under a name of your choice.

Mr J Robinson
39 Fair Tree Lane
OSWESTRY
Shropshire

Dear Mr Robinson

I thank you for your letter which I received last week.

I was interested to learn of your opinion regarding the inefficient and antiquated method of recording the details of a customer's credit card. You state that the act of drawing a weighted lever over the card in order to reproduce an impression of the embossed letters and numbers has connotations of carving initials into stone or writing in wax using a quill pen—both of which are charmingly time-wasting.

It is with great pleasure therefore that I enclose the illustrated leaflet which gives details of a new card recorder. As you will see the card is inserted into an attachment on the electronic cash keeper. Once in the slot the machine automatically types the details of the card on to a duplicated receipt together with the total amount of purchases. The duplicated receipt is presented to the customer for signature and a copy is kept by the retailer. This concludes the transaction. The same principle, Mr Robinson—I am sure you will agree—but somewhat streamlined.

If you would like our representative to call on you to demonstrate this attachment please complete the enclosed tear-off slip. A reply paid envelope is enclosed.

Yours faithfully

Enc

Exercise 50B

Recall the letter to Mr. Robinson, and using the search and replace facility, change 'I' to 'we'.

Remember to proof-read your work because other words may need to be changed as a result of this amendment.

Print out a hard copy.

7.3 Page Length

Most systems will allow 54 or 55 lines to be typed, and this in word processing terms constitutes a page. On some systems this page has to be saved before the next one can begin, on others a page divider is inserted and the operator can scroll up and down, back and forth. The best analogy of this is to think of a large roll of kitchen paper which is separated by perforations but which can be unrolled whenever it is needed. If the system uses a 'paging method' in which each page has to be saved before the next one can begin, then the difference is that instead of the page appearing as one long sheet, separated by perforations, the perforations have already been separated and they now appear on top of each other.

The operator has the option of changing the preset video page by changing the format settings. A page length of 54 or 55 lines allows for the top and bottom margin of approximately 6 lines each making a total of 12 line spaces in all which when added to 54 comes to 66 lines. A sheet of A4 paper holds 70 lines of text from the top edge of the paper to the bottom. This figure of 66 therefore gives a margin of tolerance which allows for any insertions to be accommodated.

If the text being typed reaches line 55 and a page break is indicated but there are only 2 or 3 lines left to type then it is possible to extend the vertical setting by calling up the appropriate menu and extending the video page or alternatively pressing a format key followed by the number of lines required e.g. 60 and extending the page to 60 lines.

7.4 Dividing the Text into Pages

Word processing systems vary more in operation in this area than any other. The following is a generalised overview of what is meant by the terms 'pagination' and 'repagination'.

Pagination refers to the splitting up of the text into a number of lines which, when printed out, will fit on to a particular size of paper (usually A4).

Many word processing programs have commands built into them which count the number of lines of type and the number of blank lines between the text, starting at the top of the screen. When a certain number of lines has been used (on average between 54 and 56), a page marker is displayed on the screen indicating to the operator that the text will break into another page at this point.

Since the program, unlike the operator, is merely counting lines, it does not take into account the appearance of the text before it places a page marker. The page marker may be so positioned that the text is split immediately before the last line of a paragraph, and takes this on to the next page. This is known as an 'orphan line' and does not assist the reader of the text. Wherever possible orphan lines are avoided in typescript. The same principle applies if the maximum page length is reached when only the first line of a paragraph has been typed, this is known as a 'widow line' and again should be avoided. Ideally, the text should be split between paragraphs, but if a paragraph has to be split, then it should be split in the middle.

Although page breaks may occur automatically on some systems depending upon the word processing program, they may not always appear where the operator would choose to place them. Therefore on many systems there is the facility to override this command and the operator can scroll through the text, which appears on the screen as one long continuous piece, with the top half falling off to accommodate the text below it, and place page markers where they are needed.

Other systems allow the operator to decide where to place the page markers in the first place. In setting up the page length, the operator may choose to type a specific number of lines on a page and may enact a command to end the page at a certain point.

After editing a document, the original page endings may change because text has been inserted or deleted. Therefore, although the program may take care of this by ending pages after a specific number of lines of type, the endings may occur in the middle of a table of figures so that half the table appears on one page and the other half appears on the next page, whereas it should really appear all on one page.

The following examples show how sales figures can be split when a page break occurs in the middle of them and how to avoid this when it is printed.

```
SALES FIGURES FOR THE MONTHS OF JANUARY, FEBRUARY AND MARCH

JANUARY    FEBRUARY    MARCH

30,000     50,000      45,000

45,000     25,000      10,000
```

```
20,000     15,000      12,000
```

```
SALES FIGURES FOR THE MONTHS OF JANUARY, FEBRUARY AND MARCH

JANUARY    FEBRUARY    MARCH

  30,000     50,000      45,000

  45,000     25,000      10,000

  20,000     15,000      12,000
```

Repagination

After editing, the operator should scroll through the text and if a page has been split where it is inappropriate they should take out the page markers and reposition them in the required place. The term used to describe this is 'repagination'.

Mention was made earlier of systems varying in operation of this facility. Some programs will automatically place page markers after a certain number of lines have been used, indicating this on the screen by a broken line appearing. Other systems may have the same built-in facility but may not show this in the same way. In addition, the machine may default (return to a preset number of lines), unless otherwise instructed.

After insertions and deletions to text have been made, the page markers will, on some systems, automatically move to accommodate these. On others it may be necessary to press a function key to repaginate the whole document, i.e. to move text from page 2 to page 3 etc.

On other systems, the automatic page markers appearing on the screen may remain in the position inserted, but the operator may call up a menu and an instruction can be given to keep all lines above and below a certain line number together. For example, if a table of figures begins at line 50 on the screen and ends at line 60 and the page marker comes in the middle of this, then an instruction can be given to keep all text below line 50 and above line 60 together.

In order to illustrate this the following diagrams represent a four-page report. Each paragraph has been given a letter so that the reader can easily see which paragraphs have been deleted and which text has been moved up following repagination.

Before editing or repaging.

After editing but before repaging: note paragraph E has been deleted.

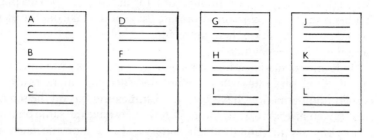

After editing and after repaging: note paragraph E has been deleted and after repaging paragraph G has been moved from page 3 to page 2.

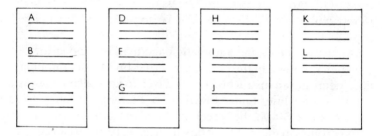

7.5 Page Numbering

Page numbering should not be confused with the terms pagination and repagination. Page numbering means literally the facility of a word processing program to number pages automatically.

It would be time-consuming to type the number of the page at the top, or at the foot of each page and, after editing, to have to renumber the pages. Therefore, some word processing systems allow the operator to first decide where the number should be placed, either at the top or at the bottom of the page, and then give a command which will start to number the pages at number one, unless instructed to start at a different number. The sheets follow on consecutively from the first number typed.

If the pages are numbered one to five and after insertions and deletions the document becomes one page longer, then, depending upon the sophistication of the word processing system, page six will automatically be numbered page six since this is the next consecutive number.

Exercise 51A

Type the following letter to the General Trading Company, Wellington Avenue, Oldham, OL8 1AB and save on disk.

Dear Sirs,

We notice from our records that two years ago you purchased four stand-alone word processors. We are now writing to inform you of an update to our software.

In order to gain the full benefit of this new software, we feel that your staff will need two or three hours training. Unfortunately, due to rising costs we do have to charge a nominal fee of £25 per person. If you wish us to provide training for your staff, then we should be pleased if you would complete the enclosed tear-off slip and return it as soon as possible showing the dates and times when training could be carried out.

Yours faithfully,

ADC COMPUTERS LTD.

— —

Please return to ADC COMPUTERS LTD, Parkland Street, Manchester.

NAME OF COMPANY....................................

DATE AND TIME MOST SUITABLE.....................

SIGNED ....

DATE...

Exercise 51B

Recall the letter addressed to the General Trading Company and paginate so that the tear-off slip appears on a separate sheet of paper. Print out a hard copy of the letter and also of the tear-off slip.

Exercise 52A

Using a 1″ margin either side and double line spacing, type the following report and save on disk.

REPORT ON THE ANNUAL GENERAL MEETING
RALLYVALE TENNIS CLUB
held on 29th October

The club secretary reported that during the year the funds had grown substantially due in part to the social events which had proved a success not only in financial terms but also in attracting new members to the club.

He paid a very special tribute to the new social secretary Miss Brentwood whose innovative ideas and excellent organisation had helped to achieve this success.

Members can see for themselves the increase in funds by examining the Income and Expenditure account.

Members are requested to pay special attention to the items of expenditure which have been purchased this year, bearing in mind that such items are not shown on the receipts and payments account. Therefore members should not be surprised to see a very much lower figure for the income over expenditure, than the surplus on the receipts and payments account, when they realise that £300 was spent upon the purchase of a personal computer.

Contrary to some reports being made that the Chairman of the club is a computer enthusiast and that is why the machine was bought, the decision to buy was in fact a committee decision and the introduction of this computer has helped to streamline the clerical functions of the club and as a result has considerably reduced the time and effort spent by the treasurer in computing the accounts, the word processing package has been particularly helpful to the secretaries in so far as they can now circularise members to inform them of forthcoming social events. It is also used for checking on those members whose subscriptions are in arrears.

Exercise 52B

Recall the Report on Rallyvale Tennis Club and carry out the corrections shown. Change the whole document to single line spacing.

Repage to a line count of 30 lines per page but ensure that the income and expenditure account is not split between the pages, i.e. all the account should appear on one page.

REPORT ON THE ANNUAL GENERAL MEETING

RALLYVALE TENNIS CLUB

held on 29th October

The club secretary reported that during the year the funds had grown *accumulated* substantially due in part to the social events which had proved a success not only in financial terms but also in attracting new members to the club.

He paid a very special tribute to the new social secretary Miss Brentwood *Julia* whose innovative ideas and excellent organisation *al ability* had helped to achieve this success.

Members can see for themselves the increase in funds by examining the Income and Expenditure account.

OPERATOR - *✱ INSERT Income & Expenditure Account - here capital*

Members are requested to pay special attention to the items of expenditure *capital* which have been purchased this year, bearing in mind that such items are not shown on the receipts and payments account. Therefore members should not be surprised to see a very much lower figure for the income over expenditure, than the surplus on the receipts and payments account, when they realise that £300 was spent upon the purchase of a personal computer.

Contrary to some reports being made ᴧ that the Chairman ~~of the club~~ is a [margin: h ⅃] [insert above: in the club]

computer enthusiast and that is why the machine was bought, ᴧ the decision to [margin: ⅃] [insert above: it should be noted that]

buy was in fact a committee decision and the introduction of this computer

has helped to streamline the clerical functions of the club and as a result

has considerably reduced the time and effort spent by the treasurer in [margin: u.c.:] [under treasurer: ‗]

computing the accounts ⁄ the word processing package has been particularly [margin: .c. ol] [under: =]

helpful to ~~the~~ secretaries ~~in so far~~ as they can now circularise members to [margin: ol] [insert above: both] [insert above: both]

inform them of forthcoming social events. ᴧ ~~It is also~~ used for checking on [margin: ⅃] [insert above: The data base on the computer is]

those members whose subscriptions are in arrears.

EXPENDITURE		INCOME	
RENT	100	SUBSCRIPTIONS	165
SECRETARY'S' HONORARIUM	52	DONATIONS	12
WAGES	208	PROCEEDS OF GALA DAY	325
ELECTRICITY	90	INTEREST ON INVESTMENTS	4
REPAIRS	25	PROFIT ON DISCO	91
REFRESHMENTS	4		
	479		
EXCESS OF INCOME OVER EXPENDITURE	120		
	597		597

Exercise 53A

Type the following using double line spacing and paginate to a line count of 25 lines per page. Save on disk. Call the document 'Integration'.

INTEGRATION OF THE OFFICE SYSTEMS

The internal organisation of most offices often dictates that each person has a specific job to do and as a result one person often performs the same task over and over again. There is a tendency therefore to think that everyone works in isolation and not as a team, and each needs a specific machine or set of information in order to do their job efficiently. However, the secretary uses the same set of records and files as the executives within the organisation. It is the purposes for which they use the records which differ.

The secretary or clerk assists in keeping the records up to date by adding or deleting data daily but they refer to the same files for reference purposes when extracting information in order to transfer it to another source. The professional, however, uses exactly the same set of records for analysis in order to monitor events and control operations or plan future actions. Therefore it is important that all records are transparent. By transparent we mean that unless designated confidential—as possibly the director's remuneration may be—the records should be accessible to all personnel.
Even the needs of a first level word processing operator and those of a word processing secretary will differ. Whilst the word processing operator may use her machine for text editing and purely word processing functions, the word processing secretary may need to use the organisation's records in order to send a memo electronically to other branch offices or to distribute half yearly sales figures to all the company's representatives on their home computer in their individual houses. She may even need to distribute information internationally using the Teletex service. A fully integrated computerised system, whilst still offering all the advantages of a dedicated word processor, will allow the operator to communicate via her console with Prestel, the public viewdata system in the U.K. which provides subscribers with up-to-date information on exchange rates and share movements.

The word processing secretary linked into the fully integrated system will be in a position to use the time management system when arranging meetings. Time management systems allow executives to keep their personal diaries on the computer system. It is possible therefore to see when each executive is available for board meetings or other group activities assisting in the interaction of the company's key personnel. A word processing secretary working for the personnel officer may need to access the payroll on the main system in order to ascertain information regarding the number of personnel earning over a specific figure for inclusion in a report on salaries. As the word processor is part of the whole system, this can be done via the word processing work station.

At one time word processing was seen as a separate function from computing. Now it is recognised that the performance of word processing tasks require specifically designed software and in ideal circumstances hardware. It is nevertheless an integral part of the computerised system and its files should be linked to all the others. The other main elements of the computerised system comprise data base management, communications facilities and accounting software with spread sheet software to assist all calculating processes.

Even though word processing needs to· be integrated into this system it does not mean that the word processing operator has to tolerate the inconvenience of using a system which was primarily designed for computing, but into which the programmers deigned to include some text editing facilities. For word processing to be successful it is necessary that although integrated into the main system where all the central records are stored, possibly on a main frame computer, the software and hardware can be designed with the functions of a typist in mind. Therefore it is the various consoles which will differ in appearance. Rather than a number of isolated work stations all performing their own functions, i.e. a personal computer for the manager which does not perform word processing, because he does not need it, and a large main frame calculating the wages on a weekly one-off operation, the whole of the office information system is open to all work stations whether these be stand alone word processors or personal computers. To work properly all must be able to communicate with each other through the central record keeping centre.

Exercise 53B Repagination

Recall the document entitled 'Integration' and carry out the corrections shown.

Change to single line spacing and repaginate to 45 lines per page, taking care not to leave orphan or widow lines.

INTEGRATION OF THE OFFICE SYSTEMS

The internal organisation of most offices often dictates that each person has a specific job to do and as a result one person often performs the same task over and over again. There is a tendency therefore to think that everyone works in isolation and not as a team, and each needs a specific machine or set of information in order to do their job efficiently.   However, the secretary uses the same set of records and files as the executives within the organisation. It is the purposes for which they use the records which differ.

The secretary or clerk assists in keeping the records up to date by adding or deleting data ~~daily~~ but they refer to the same files for reference purposes when extracting information in order to transfer it to another source.   The professional, however, uses exactly the same set of records for analysis in order to monitor events and control operations or plan future actions. Therefore it is important that all records are transparent. By 'transparent' we mean that, unless designated confidential - as possibly the director's remuneration may be - the records should be accessible to all personnel.

Only in this way do systems work because systems rely upon the interaction of people to perform different roles. Office automation assists this.

Even the needs of a first level word processing operator and those of a word processing secretary will differ. Whilst the word processing operator may use her machine for text editing and purely word processing fuctions, the word processing secretary may need to use the organisation's records in order to send a memo electronically to other branch offices or to distribute half yearly sales figures to all the company's representatives on their home computers ~~in their individual houses.~~ She may even need to distribute information internationally using the Teletex service. A fully integrated computerised system, whilst still offering all the advantages of a dedicated word processor, will allow the operator to communicate via her console with Prestel, the public viewdata system in the U.K. which provides subscribers with up-to-date information on exchange rates and share movements.

The word processing secretary linked into the fully integrated system will be in a position to use the time management system when arranging meetings. Time management systems allow executives to keep their personal diaries on the computer system. It is possible therefore to see when each executive is available for board meetings or other group activities, which aid ~~assisting~~ in the interaction of the company's key personnel. A word processing secretary working for the personnel officer may need to access the payroll on the main system in order to ascertain information regarding the number of personnel earning over a specific figure for inclusion in a report on salaries. As the word processor is part of the whole system, this can be done via the word processing work station.

Not long ago ~~At one time~~ word processing was seen as a separate function from computing. Now it is recognised that ~~the performance of~~ word processing tasks require specifically designed software and in ideal circumstances hardware. It is nevertheless an integral part of the computerised system and its files should be linked to all the others. ~~The other main elements of the computerised system comprise data base management, communications facilities and accounting software with spread sheet software to assist all calculating processes.~~

¶/ Even though word processing needs to be integrated into ~~this~~ *the* system it does
not mean that the word processing operator has to tolerate the inconvenience
of using a system which was primarily designed for computing, but into which
the programmers deigned to include some text editing facilities. For word
processing to be successful it is necessary that although integrated into the
main system where all the central records are stored, possibly on a main
frame computer, the software and hardware can be designed with the functions
and needs
of a typist in mind. Therefore it is the various consoles which will differ
in appearance. Rather than a number of isolated work stations all performing
their own functions, i.e. a personal computer for the manager ~~which does not~~
~~perform word processing, because he does not need it,~~ and a large main frame
as in batch processings
calculating the wages on a weekly one-off operation, the whole of the office
information system is open to all work stations whether these be stand alone
word processors or personal computers. To work properly all must be able to
communicate with each other through the central record keeping centre.

Test Yourself

1 What do you understand by a 'standard letter'?
2 What do you understand by the term 'list'?
3 How is a list created?
4 What is 'mail merge' or 'list processing' as used in word
   processing?
5 What is an 'orphan line'?
6 What do you understand by the term 'pagination'?
7 Why is it sometimes necessary for the operator to specify the
   number of lines which are typed on one page?
8 Give three examples when an operator would use the search
   and replace facility.
9 Give two examples when the mail merge facility would be used
   in a general office.

10 What do you understand by the term 'repagination'?

PART VII

APPLICATIONS OF WORD PROCESSING

Chapter 8

The Applications of Word Processing in Various Organisations

8.1 The Applications of a Word Processor in the Office of a Local Authority

Minutes of council meetings

Local government in Britain is run by representatives who have been elected by the people of the town or county. These representatives are the council members.

Before major decisions are taken in the various departments of local government, such as Housing, Finance, Education, Leisure Services and many others, a meeting is held with representatives of that department, i.e. local government officers and council members serving on that committee. A written record of what took place at that meeting (minutes of the meeting) is taken and this is usually typed in a draft format and circulated to all members who were present at the meeting. The secretary of the committee often makes amendments to these drafts and returns them to the word processing unit, where the minutes, which have been saved on disk, are recalled and the alterations carried out. The minutes are then returned to the secretary and only the alterations need to be checked, not the whole document— as would be the case if the minutes had been completely retyped using a conventional typewriter.

Register of electors

As the name implies, this is a register which lists the names and addresses of persons residing in a particular geographical area, who are entitled to vote. The population constantly changes because young people reach the age of 18 and therefore are eligible to vote for the first time and their names need to be added to the list. People pass away and their names need to be deleted from the list. People also move in and out of the area, so the residents one year are not the same the next year. Therefore the register of electors requires constant revisions by way of insertions and deletions. A word processor is ideal for this purpose.

Postal votes

Where postal votes are required for persons who are unable to attend a polling station at the time of elections, names and addresses can be extracted from the register of electors and printed on to sticky labels or envelopes ready for posting.

Expenditure budgets

Financial planning requires that items of expected expenditure are listed at the beginning of the financial year. At the end of the financial year the actual figures of expenditure are entered and compared to the forecast figure. The difference between these two is known as a variance. A word processor is particularly useful in the preparation of such sheets, where the headings are presented on a tabulated sheet. These headings consist of items of expenditure which rarely change, but the figures entered under them constantly change. The tabulated sheets can be saved on disk and last year's figures deleted and this year's figures entered, or alternatively, this year's figures can be added and serve as a basis of comparison with last year's expenditure statement.

Loans and interest payments

Since local authorities are borrowers and lenders of money certain legal contracts need to be prepared, for instance if the local authority has granted a mortgage to a citizen then a contract will be prepared and presented to the mortgagee, setting out the terms and conditions of the agreement. Standard paragraphs which are common to all such contracts can be saved on disk and a specific document can be drawn up using these, with only the variable items, such as the names of the parties concerned and the amounts involved, having to be entered separately.

8.2 The Applications of a Word Processor in a College

The College prospectus

College prospectuses are published annually. Their function is to give a list of proposed courses, together with the college calendar, various conditions regarding attendance and assessment requirements of students and also the names and qualifications of staff members.

Since there are movements in staff, as well as changes to their status and also in some cases to their qualifications, this list needs to be annually updated. A word processor will prove ideal for such a purpose, as it will also when revisions are made to the course programs and new courses are offered.

Other college literature

As well as the college prospectus setting out details of courses available, different faculties or departments tend to produce leaflets for promotional activities. These may promote specific courses, such as short refresher courses for adults, or computer literacy courses or any other such areas where the current trends are catered for. These leaflets can be produced on a word processor and then using the listing and merging facility mailed to the considered 'target market', e.g. local industries and commercial organisations.

Profiles on students

With the continuing need to keep assessment registers upon the progress of individuals to satisfy the criteria specified by sponsoring bodies, such as the Manpower Services Commission, and by examination boards (in the case of assessment by assignment programmes), word processors can prove an adequate means of keeping the file data up to date, with additions being made quickly and efficiently on disk, ready for the production of hard copies if these are required.

Statistical information

Student numbers play an important part in the record keeping of a college and affect such items as capital and revenue expenditure and allowances and also the designated grading of the college. Therefore records must be kept of the number of students attending particular courses. These can easily be entered upon tabulated sheets, ready prepared on disk in cases where the courses may remain relatively static from year to year but where the student numbers will fluctuate.

Work sheets and lecture notes

These of necessity must be updated at least annually, if not more often. Therefore the production of these in draft enables the lecturer to see the finished article and make any necessary amendments before it is finally printed.

8.3 The Applications of a Word Processor in the Estate Agent's Office

The bulk of the typing which is carried out in an estate agent's office is that of house or property specifications, containing descriptions of the properties for sale.

Standard phrases

A word processor can be used for the initial typing of these specifications, many of which will have the same features, e.g:

'situated in a much sought after location'
'open aspect'
'good decorative order'
'viewing by appointment through the Agents'.

As well as these standard phrases, which can be saved on disk and used as library documents, a general format for the specification can also be saved on disk. An example is the side headings which are used:

INTERNAL FEATURES

GROUND FLOOR

Kitchen

Lounge

Dining Room

FIRST FLOOR

Master Bedroom

Second Bedroom

Price

Rateable Value

These can be moved around the specification according to the format required.

Estate agents also produce much advertising copy for the local newspapers. This usually consists of an abridged version of all the specifications of the properties which are given out to the clients. These same abridged descriptions could be used to send to clients who are on the mailing list, giving them details of the houses for sale in a particular area. The mailing list forms the envelope list also, so that address labels can be produced using the listing and merging facility.

Depending upon the sophistication of the word processing program, it may be possible to sort and extract houses which match a certain criteria, e.g. houses within a particular price range of £30,000 to £50,000, of a particular type (detached) and size (three bedrooms) in a certain area (Maidenhead). As well as extracting all of these features, again depending upon the word processing program, it may be possible to place the houses containing these features, into descending or ascending order of price.

Standard letters

Using the listing and merging facility standard letters can be sent to potential clients, asking them if they want their names to be retained on the mailing list, so as to eliminate the unnecessary expense of sending house details to clients who are no longer interested in purchasing a house.

8.4 The Applications of a Word Processor in a Hospital

Any organisation has a bank of information relating to the product or service it is offering. In service 'industries' the information on record consists of details of the client, the consumer, or in the case of hospitals, the patient.

Fortunately the people who enter a hospital one year are not those who enter the next year, or the next month or week for that matter, so the records kept are constantly changing. The introduction of a word processor means that for the duration of the time that a patient is under the hospital's care, their name and address and personal details need only be recorded once and this will form the basis of the 'static information'. Any details which change, such as the treatment they receive or the results of medical investigations conducted upon them, can be added to their record and this can be quickly updated.

Provided the computing system in use in the hospital is sophisticated enough, the same records which are kept for word processing can be used for data processing. For instance, if the patient's age is recorded on the records, it is a simple computing task to do a statistical analysis upon the age ranges of patients admitted. The same statistical analysis can be applied to a range of diseases or ailments from which the patients have suffered. In this instance it would be necessary to first code and categorise the ailments, possibly very broadly into medical and surgical cases, then these would be subdivided into subjects such as obstetrics, or heart- and lung-associated diseases; the subdivisions are endless.

A decision as to what information is required and for what purposes it will be used will need to be undertaken by the hospital management team, but this example is given to illustrate the fact that word processing is only part of an integrated system of total record-keeping.

Standard letters and standard forms

All patients entering the hospital are eventually discharged. Many require follow-up letters requesting them to attend the out-patients' department some six weeks after their discharge. A standard letter can be prepared into which the day, date and time of the appointment, and the consultant's name can be incorporated. The patient's record should already contain the other variables, such as their name and address.

The letter sent to patients calling them for admission for an operation can be a standard letter. Again the only variables which need to be changed will be the date and time of admission and the name of the ward to which they are being admitted.

Included with this letter can be a printed form, showing the times of visiting hours, which the patient can give to his relatives. This form also can be produced upon the word processor so if any variations occur, and visiting times differ from the normal times, for instance during the Christmas holidays, these amendments need only be added.

Internal correspondence and staff notices

A hospital, like any large organisation, will have many staff, and a communications system to keep them informed of changes will be necessary. In this type of establishment, where peoples' lives depend upon the employees within, rules and regulations are very important. To ensure that all staff are aware of current regulations, such as procedures in the event of emergencies, or new Government legislation regarding the prescribing and administering of drugs, it is necessary that this communication is given in writing as well as verbally. A word processor enables the production of such staff notices much more quickly than a typing and printing process. Also any changes can be undertaken in the event of a new regulation being introduced, at short notice.

8.5 The Applications of a Word Processor in a Doctor's Surgery

Patient appointment schedules

A list of all appointments for the day can be compiled and saved on disk. The following sequence of events serves to illustrate the use of this.

The sick person telephones the surgery asking for an appointment with the doctor. The medical receptionist will have on the screen, in the early morning, a list of all the doctors and times of appointments available. These may be in 'windows', i.e. divisions on the screen, and each window will be a separate list for each of the doctors in the practice. The patient requests an appointment for 1500 hours that day with Dr. Jones. The medical receptionist checks the 'window' with Dr. Jones's appointments and, providing this time is available, types in the patient's name. The disk containing the appointments is then updated and provides all the details of the day's appointments for each doctor.

Patient records

If patients' records are kept on disk, the medical receptionist, upon receiving a request from a patient for an appointment, will be in a position to call up on disk the patient's record, which will contain their medical history. This can be printed out ready for the doctor when a visit to the patient is made.

Updating patient records

Once the doctor has actually visited the patient and made notes on the hard copy regarding the symptoms, investigations or treatment suggested, diagnosis or prognosis, the receptionist can then update the patient's record on disk and add the date of the visit.

Standard forms

A patient may be referred by the general practitioner to a hospital consultant. The medical receptionist recalls a standard form from disk. The form is a request for a hospital appointment and needs to be completed with the details of the patient, such as the name and address and a brief synopsis of the reason for the referral. A hard copy of this form can then be sent to the hospital, or alternatively this could be sent to the hospital directly from screen to screen if the hospital and the doctor share a local area network.

Results of investigations

Following a patient's visit to the hospital pathology laboratory the results of tests (such as blood tests, etc.) performed, can be transmitted directly to the general practitioner, again via a local area network. The results can be transferred to the patient's record on disk after the doctor has seen them, or alternatively printed on to a hard copy and passed to the doctor, in preparation for the patient's next visit.

8.6 The Applications of Word Processing in Hotel Management

Guest information sheets

These are often distributed to guests upon their arrival. The standard information which guests require include such items as:

the times when the restaurant is open,
the opening and closing times of the coffee shop,
the procedure for booking tennis or squash courts,
the times when the solarium or sauna are open,
the arrangement for early morning alarm calls,
the procedures for payment of accounts,
the dates when the roof-top garden restaurant opens.

All this information, although relatively static, does occasionally need revising. Therefore it can be saved on disk and if the times of the roof-top restaurant opening vary according to the season of the year, then this item can be quickly deleted, and the up-to-date sheets reproduced.

Menus

Of necessity the menus presented by hotels will vary each day, therefore with the co-operation of the chef, a list of all the dishes which are regularly served can be typed and saved on disk. These may be categorised by courses, such as the first course menus, the main course menus and the dessert menus. Once the chef has decided what to offer each day or week, the hotel receptionist can select the items from the prepared composite lists on disk and assemble these together to form the menu. This is a particularly useful word processing function if the menu is prepared in two or more languages, because a ready-prepared translation can be also saved on disk and this removes the necessity of painstakingly typing in a foreign language each time.

Standard forms

Many hotels offer chauffeur-driven services to and from the airports. Therefore a standard form is prepared using the word processor and completed on the screen at the time of the guest's request. The exact time of the early morning calls, together with the type of breakfast requirements, i.e. full English breakfast or continental, the time of arrival of the car, the flight number and destination, can all be keyed in by the receptionist whilst the guest is present and then a hard copy printed out and given to the guest to sign, after checking the details. This provides a service and removes the chore of the guest having to complete the form themselves and perhaps omitting certain details.

Preparation of notices

All notices for public display can be prepared on the word processor and these can be made to look attractive by using enhanced printing or line drawing; on some systems a program is available whereby artwork can be produced.

The notices may include such details as the telephone numbers of the local taxi services, or the times of public transport or flight times to and from the provincial airports to major cities. All these notices can be saved on disk and updated quickly if changes occur.

Entertainment programmes

In hotels which cater for the holiday trade, a list showing arranged events, such as a fancy dress party or a barbecue night can be produced and updated to include local events or excursions which may coincide with national events and holidays, an example being the 'Battle of Flowers' which is held annually in Jersey or 'Thanksgiving' which is celebrated in the U.S.A.

Glossary of Terms Used in Word Processing

Abandon Document   To stop editing, saving or printing a document

Access   To gain entry to the system or a document

Bi-directional Printing   Printing in both directions

Block Codes   A marker which appears in the form of a small square block on the screen which denotes where variables will be inserted into a standard letter. This marker is often achieved by pressing a special function key or a combination of keys i.e. the code key and a letter on the keyboard, depending upon the word processing system used. On some systems the ampersand sign is used or angle brackets instead.

Block Column Move   To move a block of typescript to another place

Boiler Plating   Building up a document from stored phrases

Booting Up   Programming the system

Bold Print   Print which is darker than the rest of the typescript

Centring   Positioning text in the centre of a page, usually horizontally

Character   A letter, number or symbol on the keyboard

Command   An instruction to the word processor, made by using certain function keys

Communications   One word processor talking to another, screen to screen. This often involves net-working the work stations, which means connecting them together by cables so that information can be transferred between them.

Concurrent Printing   Printing from disk, whilst the screen is being used to produce another document

Console   The unit which houses the screen, VDU

Control Key   A key used often in conjunction with another to perform certain functions

Cursor   The typing point denoted by a marker on the screen. Its shape varies according to the system. Sometimes this marker flashes.
Cut and Paste   To take text from one place and position it in another part of the same document, or to take text from one document and position it in another one

Decimal Tab   A tabular stop which lines up the decimal points
Dedicated Word Processor   Computer equipment which is purpose-built for word processing only
Default   The preset conditions or values, e.g. margin settings, to which, unless otherwise instructed, the program reverts
Delete   To remove a character, or piece of text from the screen
Direct Access   The ability to gain entry into another part of the computing system
Directory   The list of the contents on a disk
Double Column Layout   Text displayed in two narrow columns across a page
Draft Printing   Using a printer function which gives a lower quality finish, often used for work which will be edited before the final copy is produced

Electronic Mail   Mail which is sent electronically, i.e. transferred from one machine to another over external telephone lines. The sender indicates a specific machine for receipt of the document.
Embedded   Contained within, e.g. within the printer's programme
Embolden   To overstrike the characters to give the type a bold print
Exit   To leave a document, or the system

Format   The layout of a document
Format Line   The line at the top of the screen showing margin settings, and tabular settings
Function Keys   The keys which make the machine perform a certain operation. Often these keys are additional to the alphabetic or numerical keys on the keyboard.

Graphics   The operation where horizontal and vertical lines can be drawn on the screen, used to draw tables, etc.

Hard Copy   The print-out
Hardware   The physical pieces of equipment, i.e. disk drives, printers, and the VDU
Highlight   A piece of text which appears brighter than the rest, usually after a command has been given to move a line, etc. This is to indicate to the operator the line which is being moved.

Incremental Spaces   The spaces left between words so that the right-hand margin may appear straight, i.e. justified. Depending upon the length of the words the machine will adjust the spaces between them so that they appear equal.

Index   A list of all the document names which appear on a disk

Input   To feed data into the word processor or computer

Justification   The adjustment of the text to create a straight right-hand margin.

K—Kilobyte   One kilobyte equals 1,000 characters. The word processor's memory capacity is expressed in the number of 'K' it will hold, i.e. 64K, 128K.

Listing   The use of a word processor to select items from a list, e.g. of variable information which is later inserted into standard letters. This term is sometimes known as Listing and Merging.

Mail Merge   The facility on a word processor to merge variable information with a standard document

Memory   The capacity of the word processor to hold a certain number of K, kilobytes

Menu   The list of instructions which appears on the screen and which directs the operator to press certain function keys in order to perform particular operations

Microtype   Very small type, i.e. 15 characters to the inch

Mode   The mode of operation, e.g. insert mode or numeric mode. When a function key is pressed, the machine is put into a state in which that particular function may be carried out, for instance when in insert mode the text on the screen may drop down a line in order to accommodate any other text which needs to be inserted

Modem   An instrument which is attached to a telephone and computer and which enables computer data to be sent or received over the telephone lines

Numeric Mode   A mode of operation which lines up columns of figures by using a decimal point

Operating System   The program that looks after the general operation of the computer, e.g. displaying text on the screen, operating the disk drive and keyboard operations

Orphan Line   The last line of a paragraph of text which has been taken to a new page on its own

Pagination   A facility of a word processor which splits a long piece of text into a certain number of lines to form pages

Peripherals   Part of the word processing system, e.g. disk drives and printers

Password   A word which has to be typed in before the operator can access the system. The password is often used as a security code so that unauthorised persons who do not know it can not gain entry to the information stored on the word processor or computer.

Program   The software which makes the word processor/computer carry out the task it is designed to do

Protected Spaces   A special code typed into the space which appears between proper names, so that they remain on the same line, e.g. Mr. J. Jones

Proof-read   To check work on the screen for spelling, punctuation and typing errors before the print-out is obtained

Queue   A number of documents awaiting printing

Qwerty   The traditional typewriter keyboard which has the letters QWERTY on the left-hand side

Recall   To bring the contents of a document which has been stored on disk to the screen

Ruler Line   Another name for the format line

Save   To save text on disk; this is sometimes referred to as memorise

Scrolling   Moving the cursor from left to right and up and down the screen

Soft Copy   The screen copy as opposed to the print-out which is known as the hard copy

Software   The program; this makes the machine operate

Stand Alone Machine   A word processor or computer which is completely self-contained, with its own operating system, disk drive and printer

Systems Disk   The program disk which is loaded into the system before word processing begins

Time Management System   A device built into some word processing/computing software which enables the operator to view the diaries of certain personnel so that meetings can be planned when all members of a team are available

Update   To save alterations made on a recalled document on disk

Wraparound   The facility on a wordprocessing program whereby, when the text reaches the right-hand margin, the typing point will automatically return to the left-hand margin without the need for the operator to press the carriage return key

Widow Line   A line of type which is left behind on a previous page when the rest of the paragraph is taken to the next page

Work Disk   The disk upon which the text is saved

Index

191